Harvard Business Review

ON

THE HIGH-PERFORMANCE

ORGANIZATION

THE HARVARD BUSINESS REVIEW PAPERBACK SERIES

The series is designed to bring today's managers and professionals the fundamental information they need to stay competitive in a fast-moving world. From the preeminent thinkers whose work has defined an entire field to the rising stars who will redefine the way we think about business, here are the leading minds and landmark ideas that have established the *Harvard Business Review* as required reading for ambitious businesspeople in organizations around the globe.

Other books in the series:

Other books in the series (continued):

Harvard Business Review on Decision Making

Harvard Business Review on Developing Leaders

Harvard Business Review on Doing Business in China

Harvard Business Review on Effective Communication

Harvard Business Review on Entrepreneurship

Harvard Business Review on Finding and Keeping the Best People

Harvard Business Review on the High-Performance Organization

Harvard Business Review on Innovation

Harvard Business Review on the Innovative Enterprise

Harvard Business Review on Knowledge Management

Harvard Business Review on Leadership

Harvard Business Review on Leadership at the Top

Harvard Business Review on Leadership in a Changed World

Harvard Business Review on Leading in Turbulent Times

Harvard Business Review on Leading Through Change

Harvard Business Review on Managing Diversity

Harvard Business Review on Managing High-Tech Industries

Harvard Business Review on Managing People

Harvard Business Review on Managing Projects

Harvard Business Review on Managing Uncertainty

Harvard Business Review on Managing the Value Chain

Harvard Business Review on Managing Your Career

Harvard Business Review on Managing Yourself

Harvard Business Review on Marketing

Harvard Business Review on Measuring Corporate Performance

Harvard Business Review on Mergers and Acquisitions

Harvard Business Review on the Mind of the Leader

Harvard Business Review on Motivating People

Harvard Business Review on Negotiation and Conflict Resolution

Other books in the series (continued):

Harvard Business Review on Nonprofits

Harvard Business Review on Organizational Learning

Harvard Business Review on Strategic Alliances

Harvard Business Review on Strategies for Growth

Harvard Business Review on Supply Chain Management

Harvard Business Review on Teams That Succeed

Harvard Business Review on Top-Line Growth

Harvard Business Review on Turnarounds

Harvard Business Review on Women in Business

Harvard Business Review on Work and Life Balance

Harvard Business Review

ON

THE HIGH-PERFORMANCE

ORGANIZATION

A HARVARD BUSINESS REVIEW PAPERBACK

The *Harvard Business Review* articles in this collection are available as
individual reprints. Discounts apply to quantity purchases. For information and ordering, please contact Customer Service, Harvard Business
School Publishing, Boston, MA 02163. Telephone: (617) 783-7500 or
(800) 988-0886, 8 A.M. to 6 P.M. Eastern Time, Monday through Friday.
Fax: (617) 783-7555, 24 hours a day. E-mail: custserv@hbsp.harvard.edu.

978-1-4221-0278-7 (ISBN 13)

Library of Congress Cataloging-in-Publication Data
Harvard business review on the high-performance organization.
        p.   cm. — (The Harvard business review paperback series)
    Includes index.
    ISBN 1-4221-0278-5
    1. Organizational effectiveness.   I. Harvard Business School Press.
II. Harvard business review.   III. Series.
HD58.9.H38   2006
658.4´01—dc22   2006010628

Contents

Harvard Business Review

ON

THE HIGH-PERFORMANCE ORGANIZATION

Designing High-Performance Jobs

ROBERT SIMONS

Executive Summary

TALES OF GREAT STRATEGIES derailed by poor execution are all too common. That's because some organizations are designed to fail.

For a company to achieve its potential, each employee's supply of organizational resources should equal the demand, and the same balance must apply to every business unit and to the company as a whole. To carry out his or her job, each employee has to know the answers to four basic questions: What resources do I control to accomplish my tasks? What measures will be used to evaluate my performance? Who do I need to interact with and influence to achieve my goals? And how much support can I expect when I reach out to others for help?

The questions correspond to what the author calls the four basic *spans* of a job—control, accountability,

1

influence, and support. Each span can be adjusted so that it is narrow or wide or somewhere in between. If you get the settings right, you can design a job in which a talented individual can successfully execute on your company's strategy. If you get the settings wrong, it will be difficult for an employee to be effective.

The first step is to set the span of control to reflect the resources allocated to each position and unit that plays an important role in delivering customer value. This setting, like the others, is determined by how the business creates value for customers and differentiates its products and services. Next, you can dial in different levels of entrepreneurial behavior and creative tension by widening or narrowing spans of accountability and influence. Finally, you must adjust the span of support to ensure that the job or unit will get the informal help it needs.

You HAVE A COMPELLING PRODUCT, an exciting vision, and a clear strategy for your new business. You've hired good people and forged relationships with critical suppliers and distributors. You've launched a marketing campaign targeting high-value customers. All that remains is to build an organization that can deliver on the promise.

But implementation goes badly. Managers in the regional offices don't show enough entrepreneurial spirit. They are too complacent and far too slow in responding to customers. Moreover, it's proving very difficult to coordinate activities across units to serve large, multisite customers. Decision making is fragmented, and time to market is much longer than expected. Excessive costs are eating away at profit margins. You begin to wonder: "Have I put the wrong people in critical jobs?" But the problems are more widespread than that—in fact, they're systemic across the organization.

This tale of a great strategy derailed by poor execution is all too common. Of course, there are many possible reasons for such a failure and many people who might be to blame. But if this story reminds you of your own experience, have you considered the possibility that your organization is designed to fail? Specifically, are key jobs structured to achieve the business's performance potential? If not, unhappy consequences are all but inevitable.

In this article, I present an action-oriented framework that show you how to design jobs for high performance. My basic point is straightforward: For your business to achieve its potential, each employee's supply of organizational resources should equal his or her demand for them, and the same supply-and-demand balance must apply to every function, every business unit, and the entire company. Sounds simple, and it is. But only if you understand what determines this balance and how you can influence it.

The Four Spans of Job Design

To understand what determines whether a job is designed for high performance, you must put yourself in the shoes of your organization's managers. To carry out his or her job, each employee has to know the answer to four basic questions:

- "What resources do I control to accomplish my tasks?"

- "What measures will be used to evaluate my performance?"

- "Who do I need to interact with and influence to achieve my goals?"

- "How much support can I expect when I reach out to others for help?"

The questions correspond to what I call the four basic *spans* of a job: control, accountability, influence, and support. Each span can be adjusted so that it is narrow or wide or somewhere in between. I think of the adjustments as being made on sliders, like those found on music amplifiers. If you get the settings right, you can design a job in which a talented individual can successfully execute your company's strategy. But if you get the settings wrong, it will be difficult for any employee to be effective. I'll look at each span in detail and discuss how managers can adjust the settings. (The exhibit "The Four Spans" provides a summary.)

THE SPAN OF CONTROL

The first span defines the range of resources—not only people but also assets and infrastructure—for which a manager is given decision rights. These are also the resources whose performance the manager is held accountable for. Executives must adjust the span of control for each key position and unit on the basis of how the company delivers value to customers.

Consider Wal-Mart, which has configured its entire organization to deliver low prices. Wal-Mart's strategy depends on standardization of store operations coupled with economies of scale in merchandising, marketing, and distribution. To ensure standardization, Wal-Mart sets the span of control for store managers at the "narrow" end of the scale. Although they nominally control their stores, Wal-Mart site managers have limited decision rights regarding hours of operation, merchandising displays, and pricing. By contrast, the span of control for managers at corporate headquarters who oversee merchandising and other core operations is set at "wide." They are responsible for implementing best practices and consolidating operations to capture economies of scale. In addition to controlling purchasing, merchandising, and distribution, these managers even control the lighting and temperature at Wal-Mart's 3,500 stores by remote computer. (The settings for the two jobs are compared in the exhibit "Spans of Control at Wal-Mart.")

The Four Spans

Managers can adjust the spans of job design to create positions that are tuned for optimum performance.

Span	To narrow the span	To widen the span
	Narrow	Wide
1. Span of control	Reduce resources allocated to specific positions or units.	Allocate more people, assets, and infrastructure.
2. Span of accountability	Standardize work by using measures (either financial, such as line-item budget expenses, or nonfinancial, such as head count) that allow few trade-offs.	Use nonfinancial measures (such as customer satisfaction) or broad financial measures (such as profit) that allow many trade-offs.
3. Span of influence	Require people to pay attention only to their own jobs; do not allocate costs across units; use single reporting lines; and reward individual performance.	Inject creative tension through structures, systems, and goals—for example, cross-unit teams, dotted lines, matrix structures, stretch goals, cross-unit cost allocations, and transfer prices.
4. Span of support	Use leveraged, highly individualized rewards, and clearly single out winners and losers.	Build shared responsibilities through purpose and mission, group identification, trust, and equity-based incentive plans.

Of course, the spans of control will be set very differently in companies that follow different strategies. Consider Nestlé, a food company that reformulates its products in response to regional tastes for spices and sweets. In this "local value creation" configuration, the span of control for regional business managers is set very wide so that they have all the resources they need to customize products and respond to customers. Regional managers take responsibility for sales, product development, distribution, and manufacturing. As a consequence, the spans of control for managers back at the head office are relatively narrow, covering only logistics, the supply chain, global contracts, and accounting and finance.

THE SPAN OF ACCOUNTABILITY

The second span refers to the range of trade-offs affecting the measures used to evaluate a manager's achievements. For example, a person who is accountable for head count or specific expenses in an operating

---

Spans of Control at Wal-Mart

The spans of control for a store manager and a merchandising manager at Wal-Mart are quite different. To ensure standardization in operations, Wal-Mart gives the store manager relatively little control. To promote the implementation of best practices, the company gives the merchandising manager a "wide" setting.

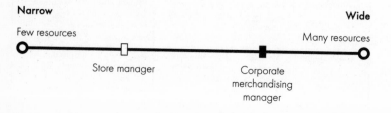

Narrow   Wide

Few resources   Many resources

Store manager   Corporate
                     merchandising
                     manager

budget can make few trade-offs in trying to improve the measured dimensions of performance and so has a narrow span of accountability. By contrast, a manager responsible for market share or business profit can make many trade-offs and thus has a relatively wide span of accountability.

Your setting for this span is determined by the kind of behavior you want to see. To ensure compliance with detailed directives, hold managers to narrow measures. To encourage creative thinking, make them responsible for broad metrics such as market share, customer satisfaction, and return on capital employed, which allow them greater freedom.

The span of control and the span of accountability are not independent. They must be considered together. The first defines the resources available to a manager; the second defines the goals the manager is expected to achieve. You might conclude, therefore, that the two spans should be equally wide or narrow. As the adage goes, authority should match responsibility. But in high-performing organizations, many people are held to broad performance measures such as brand profit and customer satisfaction, even though they do not control all the resources—manufacturing and service, for example—needed to achieve the desired results.

There is a good reason for this discrepancy. By explicitly setting the span of accountability wider than the span of control, executives can force their managerial subordinates to become entrepreneurs. In fact, entrepreneurship has been defined (by Howard H. Stevenson and J. Carlos Jarillo) as "the process by which individuals—either on their own or inside organizations—pursue opportunities without regard to the resources they currently control." What happens when employees are faced with this *entrepreneurial gap*? They must use their energy and creativity to figure out how to succeed without direct control of the resources they need. (See the exhibit "Creating the Entrepreneurial Gap.") Thus, managers can adjust these two spans to stimulate creativity and entrepreneurial behavior.

Of course, spans of accountability vary by level in most organizations—in general, they are wider at the top of a company and narrower at the bottom. The CEO of McDonald's has a wide span of accountability that encompasses stock price, earnings per share, and competitive market position. A McDonald's store manager has a much narrower span. She must focus on compliance with standard operating procedures, and she is monitored through detailed input and process measures.

THE SPAN OF INFLUENCE

The third span corresponds to the width of the net that an individual needs to cast in collecting data, probing for new information, and attempting to influence the work

Creating the Entrepreneurial Gap

By holding managers accountable for more than they control, a company can encourage entrepreneurial behavior.

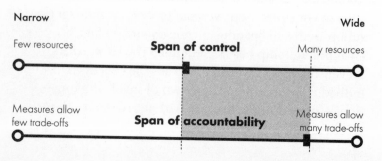

of others. An employee with a narrow span of influence does not need to pay much attention to people outside his small area to do his job effectively. An individual with a wide span must interact extensively with, and influence, people in other units.

As is the case with the other spans, senior managers can adjust the span of influence to promote desired behaviors. They can widen the span when they want to stimulate people to think outside the box to develop new ways of serving customers, increasing internal efficiencies, or adapting to changes in external markets. In many companies, widening the span of influence counteracts the rigidity of organizational structures based on boxes and silos. For example, although global companies like Procter & Gamble need to be responsive to local customers' needs, they must also create pressure for people in different operations to look beyond their silos to consolidate operations and share best practices to lower costs. Similarly, firms such as big-box retailers that centralize merchandising and distribution to deliver low prices must ensure that they continue to monitor changing competitive dynamics. Operations managers who are insulated from the marketplace must be forced to interact with people in units that are closest to customers. In all of these cases, it's up to senior managers to ensure that individuals work across organizational boundaries to test new ideas, share information, and learn.

Executives can widen a manager's span of influence by redesigning her job—placing her on a cross-functional team, for example, or giving her an assignment that requires her to report to two bosses. They can also adjust a job's span of influence through the level of goals they set. Although the *nature* of a manager's goals drives her span of accountability (by determining the trade-offs she can make), the *level*, or difficulty, drives her sphere of influence. Someone given a stretch goal will often be forced to seek out and interact with more people than someone whose goal is set at a much lower level. Finally, executives can use accounting and control systems to adjust the span of influence. For example, the span will be wider for managers who are forced to bear the burden of indirect cost allocations generated by other units, because they will attempt to influence the decisions of the units responsible for the costs.

The more complex and interdependent the job, the more important a wide span of influence becomes. In fact, a wide influence span is often an indication of both the power and effectiveness of an executive. In describing eBay's Meg Whitman, for example, A.G. Lafley, the CEO of Procter & Gamble, said, "The measure of a powerful person is that their circle of influence is greater than their circle of control."

THE SPAN OF SUPPORT

This final span refers to the amount of help an individual can expect from people in other organizational units. Again, the slider can be set anywhere from narrow to wide depending on how much commitment from others the person needs in order to implement strategy.

Jobs in some organizations—particularly positions such as commission-based sales in efficient and liquid markets—do not need wide spans of support. In fact, such organizations generally operate more efficiently with narrow spans, since each job is independent and individual contributions can be calculated easily at day's end. Traders in financial institutions, for example, need little support from their fellow traders, and their colleagues can and should stay focused on their own work (and should be compensated solely for their success in generating profit).

But wide spans of support become critically important when customer loyalty is vital to strategy implementation (for example, at exclusive hotel chains) or when the organizational design is highly complex because of sophisticated technologies and a complex value chain (in aerospace or computers, for instance). In these cases, individuals throughout the company must move beyond their job descriptions to respond to requests for help from others who are attempting to satisfy customers or navigate organizational processes.

Managers cannot adjust a job's span of support in isolation. That's because the span is largely determined by people's sense of shared responsibilities, which in turn stems from a company's culture and values. In many cases, therefore, all or most of a company's jobs will have a wide span of support, or none will. But even within a given company culture, there are often circumstances in which managers need to widen the span of support separately for key business units (for example, to support a new division created to bundle and cross sell products from other units) or for key positions (for example, to facilitate the work of cross-functional task forces).

There are various policies that managers can employ to widen spans of support. For example, a focus on a customer-based mission typically creates a sense of shared purpose. In addition, broad-based stock ownership plans and team- and group-centered incentive programs often foster a sense of equity and belonging and encourage people to help others achieve shared goals. Firms that are characterized by wide spans of support also frown on letting top executives flaunt the trappings of privilege and generally follow a policy of promoting people internally to senior positions.

The slider settings for the four spans in any job or business unit are a function of the business's strategy and the role of that job or unit in implementing it. When you are adjusting job or unit design, the first step is to set the span of control to reflect the resources allocated to each position and unit that plays an important role in delivering customer value. This setting, like the others, is determined by how the business creates value for customers and differentiates its products and services from competitors'. Next, you can dial in different levels of entrepreneurial behavior and creative tension for specific jobs and units by widening or narrowing spans of accountability and influence. Finally, you must adjust the span of support to ensure that the job or unit will get the informal help it needs.

The exhibit "Four Spans at a Software Company" displays the settings of the spans for a marketing and sales manager at a well-known company that develops and sells complex software for large corporate clients. The span of control for this job is quite narrow. As the manager stated, "To do my day-to-day job, I depend on sales, sales consulting, competency groups, alliances, technical support, corporate marketing, field marketing, and integrated marketing communications. None of these functions reports to me, and most do not even report to my group." The span of accountability, by contrast, is wide. The manager is accountable, along with others throughout the business, for revenue growth, profit, and customer satisfaction—measures that require responsiveness and a willingness to make many trade-offs.

Note that the span of influence is set somewhat wider than the span of control. To get things done, the manager has to cross boundaries and convince people in other units (whom he cannot command) to help him. So that the manager receives the help he needs, the CEO works hard to ensure that the job's span of

---

Four Spans at a Software Company

The settings for a marketing and sales manager show a relatively narrow span of control and a relatively wide span of accountability. The discrepancy indicates that the company wants the manager to be entrepreneurial. A reasonable span of influence ensures that he has a respectable level of collaboration with colleagues outside his unit to compensate for his low span of control. Company policies designed to provide a wide span of support ensure that his entrepreneurial initiatives will get a favorable response. The dotted line connecting the two spans that describe the resources available to the job (span of control and span of support) intersects with the line connecting the two spans that describe the job's demand for resources (span of accountability and span of influence). This shows that the supply of, and demand for, resources that apply to this job are in rough balance; the job has been designed to enable the manager to succeed.

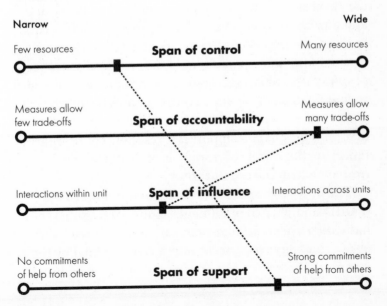

Narrow | Wide

Few resources — **Span of control** — Many resources

Measures allow few trade-offs — **Span of accountability** — Measures allow many trade-offs

Interactions within unit — **Span of influence** — Interactions across units

No commitments of help from others — **Span of support** — Strong commitments of help from others

support is wide. An ethos of mutual responsibilities has been created through shared goals, strong group identi- fication, trust, and an equity component in compensa- tion. As the manager noted, "Coordination happens because we all have customer satisfaction as our first priority. We are in constant communication, and we all are given consistent customer-satisfaction objectives."

Achieving Equilibrium

At this point, you're probably wondering how to deter- mine whether specific jobs or business units in your organization are properly designed. Jobs vary within any business, and firms operate in different markets with unique strategies. How exactly should the spans be set in these many circumstances?

After the spans have been adjusted to implement your strategy, there's an easy way to find out whether a spe- cific job is designed for high performance. It's a test that can (and should) be applied to every key job, function, and unit in your business. I'll get to the details shortly, but first, it's important to recognize the underlying nature of the four spans. Two of the spans measure the *supply* of organizational resources the company provides to individuals. The span of control relates to the level of direct control a person has over people, assets, and infor- mation. The span of support is its "softer" counterpart, reflecting the supply of resources in the form of help from people in the organization.

The other two spans—the span of accountability (hard) and the span of influence (soft)—determine the individual's *demand* for organizational resources. The level of an employee's accountability, as defined by the company, directly affects the level of pressure on him to make trade-offs; that pressure in turn drives his need for organizational resources. His level of influence, as determined by the structure of his job and the broader system in which his job is embedded, also reflects the extent to which he needs resources. As I pointed out earlier, when an employee joins a multidisciplinary initiative, or works for two bosses, or gets a stretch goal, he begins reaching out across units more frequently.

For any organization to operate at maximum efficiency and effectiveness, the supply of resources for each job and each unit must equal the demand. In other words, span of control plus span of support must equal span of accountability plus span of influence. You can determine whether any job in your organization is poised for sustained high performance—or is designed to fail—by applying this simple test: Using "Four Spans at a Software Company" as an example, draw two lines, one connecting span of control and span of support (the supply of resources) and the other connecting span of accountability and span of influence (the demand for resources).

If these two lines intersect, forming an X, as they do in the exhibit, then demand equals supply (at least roughly) and the job is properly designed for sustained performance. If the lines do not cross, then the spans are misaligned—with predictable consequences. If resources (span of control plus span of support) are insufficient for the task at hand, strategy implementation will fail; if resources are excessive, underutilization of assets and poor economic performance can be predicted.

Depending on the desired unit of analysis, this test can be applied to an individual job, a function, a business unit, and even an entire company.

When Spans Are Misaligned

Consider the case of a struggling high-tech company that makes medical devices. One division was rapidly losing revenue and market share to new competitors because of insufficient sales-force coverage and a lack of new-product development. In another division, created to bundle and cross sell products, managers were unable to get the collaboration they needed to provide a unified solution for a large potential customer. In a third, local managers were making decisions that did not support or build on the company's overall direction and strategy.

These situations arose because senior managers had failed to align the four spans for key jobs and for the divisions overall. In particular, the problems this company encountered reflect three common situations that can limit performance potential.

THE CRISIS OF RESOURCES

In some cases, the supply of resources is simply inadequate for the job at hand, leading to a failure of strategy implementation. In the medical devices company, the sales staff had neither enough people to cover the competition (a narrow span of control) nor support from R and D to bring new products to market rapidly (a narrow span of support). A crisis of resources is most likely to occur when executives spend too much time thinking about control, influence, and accountability and not enough time thinking about support. They may, for instance, set the span of accountability wider than the span of control to encourage entrepreneurial behavior. And they may set the span of influence wider than the span of control to stimulate people to interact and work across units. But if the span of support is not widened to compensate for the relatively narrow span of control, people in other units will be unwilling to help when asked.

Consider the local subsidiary of a regional investment bank. The managers had few direct resources (a narrow span of control) and relied on specialists from corporate headquarters to fly in to manage deals. Yet their span of accountability was relatively wide, with performance measures focusing on successful deals and revenue generation. Evaluations of the local managers failed to recognize or reward people's commitment to help others in the organization. As a result, the span of support was too low to support the strategy of the business, which eventually failed.

THE CRISIS OF CONTROL

Sometimes the supply of resources exceeds demand, leading to suboptimal economic performance. In highly decentralized organizations where separate business units are created to be close to customers, a crisis of control can occur when the supply of resources (the span of control plus the span of support) exceeds corporate management's ability to effectively monitor trade-offs (the span of accountability) and to ensure coordination of knowledge sharing with other units (the span of influence). The result is uncoordinated activities across units, missed opportunities, and wasted resources.

Consider a large telecommunications company in which regions were organized as independent business units. Because of rapid growth, division managers were able to create fiefdoms in which resources were plentiful. And because of the company's success, commitment to the business mission was strong. But before long, the lack of effective performance monitoring by corporate superiors caught up with the business. The strategies of the divisions often worked at cross-purposes; there was waste and redundancy. Competitors that were more focused began overtaking the units.

THE CRISIS OF RED TAPE

This can occur in any organization where powerful staff groups, overseeing key internal processes such as strategic planning and resource allocation, design performance management systems that are too complex for the organization. In such circumstances, spans of accountability and influence are very high, but resources are insufficient and misdirected. Endless time spent in staff meetings wastes resources, slows decision making, and makes the organization unable to respond rapidly to changing customer needs and competitive actions. The demand for resources exceeds supply, and strategy execution fails as more nimble competitors move in.

Adjusting the Spans over Time

Of course, organizations and job designs must change with shifting circumstances and strategies. To see how this plays out in practice, let's look at how the job spans for a typical market-facing sales unit at IBM evolved as a result of the strategic choices made by successive CEOs.

We pick up the story in 1981, when John Opel became IBM's chief executive. IBM had been organized into stand-alone product groups that were run as profit centers. Reacting to threats from Japanese companies, Opel wanted to reposition the business as a low-cost competitor. For purposes of increasing cost efficiency, the business was reorganized on a functional basis. The span of control for operating-core units such as manufacturing was widened dramatically, and there was a corresponding reduction in the spans of control and accountability for market-facing sales units (illustrated in the top panel of the exhibit "Three Eras at IBM"). The company also enlarged its definition of "customer." Rather than focus narrowly on professional IT managers in governments and large companies, IBM began marketing to small companies, resellers, and distributors. It created experimental independent business units and gave resources for experimentation without imposing any accountability for performance.

By the end of Opel's tenure, IBM was criticized for confusion about strategy and priorities. As one writer noted, "IBM settled into a feeling that it could be all things to all customers." However, the effects of these problems were masked by the dramatic and unrelenting growth of the computer industry during this period.

In 1985, John Akers took over as CEO. The organization he inherited was configured to develop, manufacture, and market computing hardware in independent silos. Not only were products incompatible across categories, they failed to meet customer needs in a world that was moving quickly from hardware to software and customer solutions. To get closer to customers, Akers created a unified marketing and services group, organized by region. The mission of this new market-facing unit was to translate customer needs into integrated product solutions and coordinate internal resources to deliver the right products to customers. Business units and divisions were consolidated into six lines of business. The span of control for the market-facing sales units widened dramatically.

The new marketing and services group was made accountable for profit, and, as a result, many new profit centers were created. Unfortunately, the existing

Three Eras at IBM

The settings for the four spans for a typical sales unit at IBM evolved as a result of the strategic choices made by successive CEOs.

John Opel

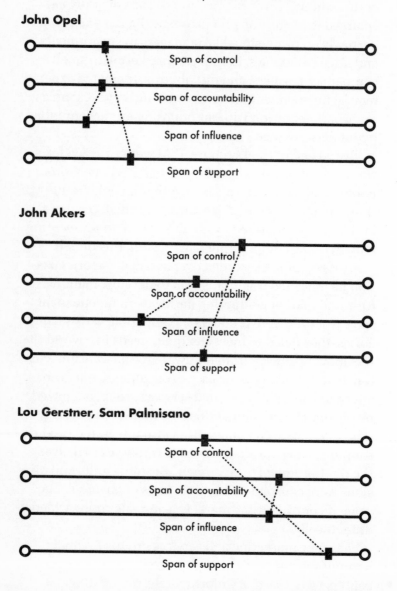

Span of control

Span of accountability

Span of influence

Span of support

John Akers

Span of control

Span of accountability

Span of influence

Span of support

Lou Gerstner, Sam Palmisano

Span of control

Span of accountability

Span of influence

Span of support

accounting system was not capable of calculating profit at the branch level or for individual customers and product lines. Instead, a top-down planning system run by centralized staff groups set sales quotas for individual product categories. Customer sales representatives thus had few choices or trade-offs; their span of accountability was not wide enough to support the company's new strategy. To make matters worse, the new profit centers made the company extremely complex and fragmented, a situation reflected in the unit's relatively narrow spans of influence and support. As the strategy's failure became evident and losses mounted, Akers considered breaking the corporation into separate entities.

Lou Gerstner took charge in 1993. He restructured the business around specific industry groups, narrowing the spans of control and widening the spans of accountability for marketing and sales units. At the same time, he widened the spans of influence by formally pairing product specialists with global industry teams, which worked closely with customers. To widen the spans of support, the company reconfigured bonuses to give more weight to corporate results than to business-unit performance.

Sam Palmisano took over as CEO in 2002 and reinforced the positive changes wrought by Gerstner. The new CEO's strategy emphasized "on-demand" computing solutions delivered through seamless integration of hardware, software, and services. This involved adopting a team-based, "dedicated service relationship" configuration at the sales units. To ensure that all employees in such a complex organization would be willing to work across units to build customer loyalty, Palmisano worked to widen spans of support further. In a well-publicized initiative, he returned the company to its roots by reemphasizing the importance of IBM values such as dedication to client success, innovation, and trust and personal responsibility in all relationships. To increase trust within the company and heighten the perception of fairness—necessary actions before people will assume responsibility for helping others—Palmisano asked the board to allocate half of his 2003 bonus to other IBM executives who would be critical leaders of the new team-based strategy.

A Precarious Balance

As IBM illustrates, complex strategies for large firms usually require that all the spans of key jobs widen, indicating high levels of both demand for, and supply of, organizational resources. But the potential for problems is great in any organization where all four spans are wide and tightly aligned. A relatively small change in any one of them will disrupt the balance of supply and demand and tip the organization toward disequilibrium. In the short run, of course, the dedication and hard work of good people can often compensate for a misalignment. But the more dynamic your markets and the more demanding your customers, the more critical and difficult it becomes to ensure that all four spans of organization design are aligned to allow your business to reach its performance potential.

Originally published in July–August 2005
Reprint R0507D

Turning Great Strategy into Great Performance

MICHAEL C. MANKINS
AND RICHARD STEELE

Executive Summary

DESPITE THE ENORMOUS TIME AND ENERGY that goes into strategy development, many companies have little to show for their efforts. Indeed, research by the consultancy Marakon Associates suggests that companies on average deliver only 63 percent of the financial performance their strategies promise.

In this article, Michael Mankins and Richard Steele of Marakon present the findings of this research. They draw on their experience with high-performing companies like Barclays, Cisco, Dow Chemical, 3M, and Roche to establish some basic rules for setting and delivering strategy:

Keep it simple, make it concrete. Avoid long, drawn-out descriptions of lofty goals and instead stick to clear language describing what your company will and won't do.

Debate assumptions, not forecasts. Create cross-functional teams drawn from strategy, marketing, and finance to ensure the assumptions underlying your long-term plans reflect both the real economics of your company's markets and its actual performance relative to competitors.

Use a rigorous analytic framework. Ensure that the dialogue between the corporate center and the business units about market trends and assumptions is conducted within a rigorous framework, such as that of "profit pools."

Discuss resource deployments early. Create more realistic forecasts and more executable plans by discussing up front the level and timing of critical deployments.

Clearly identify priorities. Prioritize tactics so that employees have a clear sense of where to direct their efforts.

Continuously monitor performance. Track resource deployment and results against plan, using continuous feedback to reset assumptions and reallocate resources.

Reward and develop execution on capabilities. Motivate and develop staff.

Following these rules strictly can help narrow the strategy-to-performance gap.

THREE YEARS AGO, the leadership team at a major manufacturer spent months developing a new strategy for its European business. Over the prior half-decade, six new competitors had entered the market, each deploying the latest in low-cost manufacturing technology and slashing prices to gain market share. The performance of the European unit—once the crown jewel of the company's portfolio—had deteriorated to the point that top management was seriously considering divesting it. To turn around the operation, the unit's leadership team had recommended a bold new "solutions strategy"—one that would leverage the business's installed base to fuel growth in after-market services and equipment financing. The financial forecasts were exciting—the strategy promised to restore the business's industry-leading returns and growth. Impressed, top management quickly approved the plan, agreeing to provide the unit with all the resources it needed to make the turnaround a reality.

Today, however, the unit's performance is nowhere near what its management team had projected. Returns, while better than before, remain well below the company's cost of capital. The revenues and profits that managers had expected from services and financing have not materialized, and the business's cost position still lags behind that of its major competitors.

At the conclusion of a recent half-day review of the business's strategy and performance, the unit's general manager remained steadfast and vowed to press on. "It's all about execution," she declared. "The strategy we're pursuing is the right one. We're just not delivering the numbers. All we need to do is work harder, work smarter."

The parent company's CEO was not so sure. He wondered: Could the unit's lackluster performance have more to do with a mistaken strategy than poor execution? More important, what should he do to get better performance out of the unit? Should he do as the general manager insisted and stay the course—focusing the organization more intensely on execution—or should he encourage the leadership team to investigate new strategy options? If execution was the issue, what should he do to help the business improve its game? Or should he just cut his losses and sell the business? He left the operating review frustrated and confused—not at all confident that the business would ever deliver the performance its managers had forecast in its strategic plan.

Talk to almost any CEO, and you're likely to hear similar frustrations. For despite the enormous time and energy that goes into strategy development at most companies, many have little to show for the effort. Our research suggests that companies on average deliver only 63 percent of the financial performance their strategies promise. Even worse, the causes of this strategy-to-performance gap are all but invisible to top management. Leaders then pull the wrong levers in their attempts to turn around performance—pressing for better execution when they actually need a better strategy, or opting to change direction when they really should focus the organization on execution. The result: wasted energy, lost time, and continued underperformance.

But, as our research also shows, a select group of high-performing companies have managed to close the strategy-to-performance gap through better planning *and* execution. These companies—Barclays, Cisco Systems, Dow Chemical, 3M, and Roche, to name a few—develop realistic plans that are solidly grounded in the underlying economics of their markets and then use the plans to drive execution. Their disciplined planning and execution processes make it far less likely that they will face a shortfall in actual performance. And, if they do fall short, their processes enable them to discern the cause quickly and take corrective action. While these companies' practices are broad in scope—ranging from unique forms of planning to integrated processes for deploying and tracking resources—our experience suggests that they can be applied by any business to help craft great plans and turn them into great performance.

The Strategy-to-Performance Gap

In the fall of 2004, our firm, Marakon Associates, in collaboration with the Economist Intelligence Unit, surveyed senior executives from 197 companies worldwide with sales exceeding $500 million. We wanted to see how successful companies are at translating their strategies into performance. Specifically, how effective are they at meeting the financial projections set forth in their strategic plans? And when they fall short, what are the most common causes, and what actions are most effective in closing the strategy-to-performance gap? Our findings were revealing—and troubling.

While the executives we surveyed compete in very different product markets and geographies, they share many concerns about planning and execution. Virtually all of them struggle to produce the financial performance forecasts in their long-range plans. Furthermore, the processes they use to develop plans and monitor performance make it difficult to discern whether the strategy-to-performance gap stems from poor planning, poor execution, both, or neither. Specifically, we discovered:

Companies rarely track performance against long-term plans. In our experience, less than 15% of companies make it a regular practice to go back and compare the business's results with the performance forecast for each unit in its prior years' strategic plans. As a result, top managers can't easily know whether the projections that underlie their capital-investment and portfolio-strategy decisions are in any way predictive of actual performance. More important, they risk embedding the same disconnect between results and forecasts in their future investment decisions. Indeed, the fact that so few companies routinely monitor actual versus planned performance may help explain why so many companies seem to pour good money after bad—continuing to fund losing strategies rather than searching for new and better options.

Multiyear results rarely meet projections. When companies do track performance relative to projections over a number of years, what commonly emerges is a picture one of our clients recently described as a series of "diagonal venetian blinds," where each year's performance projections, when viewed side by side, resemble venetian blinds hung diagonally. (See the exhibit "The Venetian Blinds of Business.") If things are going reasonably well, the starting point for each year's new "blind" may be a bit higher than the prior year's starting point, but rarely does performance match the prior year's projection. The obvious implication: year after year of underperformance relative to plan.

The venetian blinds phenomenon creates a number of related problems. First, because the plan's financial forecasts are unreliable, senior management cannot confidently tie capital approval to strategic planning. Consequently, strategy development and resource allocation become decoupled, and the annual operating plan (or budget) ends up driving the company's long-term investments and strategy. Second, portfolio management gets derailed. Without credible financial forecasts, top management cannot know whether a particular business is worth more to the company and its shareholders than to potential buyers. As a result, businesses that destroy shareholder value stay in the portfolio too long (in the hope that their performance will eventually turn around), and value-creating businesses are starved for capital and other resources. Third, poor financial forecasts complicate communications with the investment community. Indeed, to avoid coming up short at the end of the quarter, the CFO and head of investor relations frequently impose a "contingency" or "safety margin" on top of the forecast produced by consolidating the business-unit plans. Because this top-down contingency

---

The Venetian Blinds of Business

This graph illustrates a dynamic common to many companies. In January 2001, management approves a strategic plan (Plan 2001) that projects modest performance for the first year and a high rate of performance thereafter, as shown in the first solid line. For beating the first year's projection, the unit management is both commended and handsomely rewarded. A new plan is then prepared, projecting uninspiring results for the first year and once again promising a fast rate of performance improvement thereafter, as shown by the second solid line (Plan 2002). This, too, succeeds only partially, so another plan is drawn up, and so on. The actual rate of performance improvement can be seen by joining the start points of each plan (the dotted line).

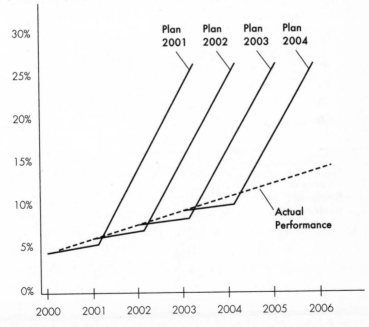

Performance
(return on capital)

is wrong just as often as it is right, poor financial forecasts run the risk of damaging a company's reputation
with analysts and investors.

A lot of value is lost in translation. Given the poor
quality of financial forecasts in most strategic plans, it is
probably not surprising that most companies fail to realize their strategies' potential value. As we've mentioned,
our survey indicates that, on average, most strategies
deliver only 63 percent of their potential financial
performance. And more than one-third of the executives
surveyed placed the figure at less than 50 percent. Put
differently, if management were to realize the full potential of its current strategy, the increase in value could be
as much as 60 percent to 100 percent!

Where the Performance Goes

*This chart shows the average performance loss implied by the importance
ratings that managers in our survey gave to specific breakdowns in the
planning and execution process.*

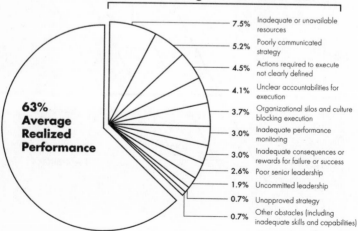

37% Average Performance Loss

7.5%	Inadequate or unavailable resources
5.2%	Poorly communicated strategy
4.5%	Actions required to execute not clearly defined
4.1%	Unclear accountabilities for execution
3.7%	Organizational silos and culture blocking execution
3.0%	Inadequate performance monitoring
3.0%	Inadequate consequences or rewards for failure or success
2.6%	Poor senior leadership
1.9%	Uncommitted leadership
0.7%	Unapproved strategy
0.7%	Other obstacles (including inadequate skills and capabilities)

63% Average Realized Performance

As illustrated in the exhibit "Where the Performance Goes," the strategy-to-performance gap can be attributed to a combination of factors, such as poorly formulated plans, misapplied resources, breakdowns in communication, and limited accountability for results. To elaborate, management starts with a strategy it believes will generate a certain level of financial performance and value over time (100 percent, as noted in the exhibit). But, according to the executives we surveyed, the failure to have the right resources in the right place at the right time strips away some 7.5 percent of the strategy's potential value. Some 5.2 percent is lost to poor communications, 4.5 percent to poor action planning, 4.1 percent to blurred accountabilities, and so on. Of course, these estimates reflect the average experience of the executives we surveyed and may not be representative of every company or every strategy. Nonetheless, they do highlight the issues managers need to focus on as they review their companies' processes for planning and executing strategies.

What emerges from our survey results is a sequence of events that goes something like this: Strategies are approved but poorly communicated. This, in turn, makes the translation of strategy into specific actions and resource plans all but impossible. Lower levels in the organization don't know what they need to do, when they need to do it, or what resources will be required to deliver the performance senior management expects. Consequently, the expected results never materialize. And because no one is held responsible for the shortfall, the cycle of underperformance gets repeated, often for many years.

Performance bottlenecks are frequently invisible to top management. The processes most companies use to develop plans, allocate resources, and track performance make it difficult for top management to discern whether the strategy-to-performance gap stems from poor planning, poor execution, both, or neither. Because so many plans incorporate overly ambitious projections, companies frequently write off performance shortfalls as "just another hockey-stick forecast." And when plans are realistic and performance falls short, executives have few early-warning signals. They often have no way of knowing whether critical actions were carried out as expected, resources were deployed on schedule, competitors responded as anticipated, and so on. Unfortunately, without clear information on how and why performance is falling short, it is virtually impossible for top management to take appropriate corrective action.

The strategy-to-performance gap fosters a culture of underperformance. In many companies, planning and execution breakdowns are reinforced—even magnified—by an insidious shift in culture. In our experience, this change occurs subtly but quickly, and once it has taken root it is very hard to reverse. First, unrealistic plans create the expectation throughout the organization that plans simply will not be fulfilled. Then, as the expectation becomes experience, it becomes the norm that performance commitments won't be kept. So commitments cease to be binding promises with real consequences. Rather than stretching to ensure that commitments are kept, managers, expecting failure, seek to protect themselves from the eventual fallout. They spend time covering their tracks rather than identifying actions to enhance performance. The organization becomes less self-critical and less intellectually honest about its shortcomings. Consequently, it loses its capacity to perform.

Closing the Strategy-to-Performance Gap

As significant as the strategy-to-performance gap is at most companies, management can close it. A number of high-performing companies have found ways to realize more of their strategies' potential. Rather than focus on improving their planning and execution processes separately to close the gap, these companies work both sides of the equation, raising standards for both planning and execution simultaneously and creating clear links between them.

Our research and experience in working with many of these companies suggests they follow seven rules that apply to planning and execution. Living by these rules enables them to objectively assess any performance shortfall and determine whether it stems from the strategy, the plan, the execution, or employees' capabilities. And the same rules that allow them to spot problems early also help them prevent performance shortfalls in the first place. These rules may seem simple—even obvious—but when strictly and collectively observed, they can transform both the quality of a company's strategy and its ability to deliver results.

Rule 1: Keep it simple, make it concrete. At most companies, strategy is a highly abstract concept—often confused with vision or aspiration—and is not something that can be easily communicated or translated into action. But without a clear sense of where the company is headed and why, lower levels in the organization cannot put in place executable plans. In short, the link between strategy and performance can't be drawn because the strategy itself is not sufficiently concrete.

To start off the planning and execution process on the right track, high-performing companies avoid long, drawn-out descriptions of lofty goals and instead stick to clear language describing their course of action. Bob Diamond, CEO of Barclays Capital, one of the fastest-growing and best-performing investment banking operations in Europe, puts it this way: "We've been very clear about what we will and will not do. We knew we weren't going to go head-to-head with U.S. bulge bracket firms. We communicated that we wouldn't compete in this way and that we wouldn't play in unprofitable segments within the equity markets but instead would invest to position ourselves for the euro, the burgeoning need for fixed income, and the end of Glass-Steigel. By ensuring everyone knew the strategy and how it was different, we've been able to spend more time on tasks that are key to executing this strategy."

By being clear about what the strategy is and isn't, companies like Barclays keep everyone headed in the same direction. More important, they safeguard the performance their counterparts lose to ineffective communications; their resource and action planning becomes more effective; and accountabilities are easier to specify.

Rule 2: Debate assumptions, not forecasts. At many companies, a business unit's strategic plan is little more than a negotiated settlement—the result of careful bargaining with the corporate center over performance targets and financial forecasts. Planning, therefore, is largely a political process—with unit management arguing for lower near-term profit projections (to secure higher annual bonuses) and top management pressing for more long-term stretch (to satisfy the board of directors and other external constituents). Not surprisingly, the forecasts that emerge from these negotiations almost always understate what each business unit can deliver in the near term and overstate what can realistically be expected in the long-term—the hockey-stick charts with which CEOs are all too familiar.

Even at companies where the planning process is isolated from the political concerns of performance evaluation and compensation, the approach used to generate financial projections often has built-in biases. Indeed, financial forecasting frequently takes place in complete isolation from the marketing or strategy functions. A business unit's finance function prepares a highly detailed line-item forecast whose short-term assumptions may be realistic, if conservative, but whose long-term assumptions are largely uninformed. For example, revenue forecasts are typically based on crude estimates about average pricing, market growth, and market share. Projections of long-term costs and working capital requirements are based on an assumption about annual productivity gains—expediently tied, perhaps, to some companywide efficiency program. These forecasts are difficult for top management to pick apart. Each line item may be completely defensible, but the overall plan and projections embed a clear upward bias—rendering them useless for driving strategy execution.

High-performing companies view planning altogether differently. They want their forecasts to drive the work they actually do. To make this possible, they have to ensure that the assumptions underlying their long-term plans reflect both the real economics of their markets and the performance experience of the company relative to competitors. Tyco CEO Ed Breen, brought in to turn the company around in July 2002, credits a revamped plan-building process for contributing to Tyco's dramatic recovery. When Breen joined the company, Tyco was a labyrinth of 42 business units and several hundred

profit centers, built up over many years through count-
less acquisitions. Few of Tyco's businesses had complete
plans, and virtually none had reliable financial forecasts.

To get a grip on the conglomerate's complex operations, Breen assigned cross-functional teams at each
unit, drawn from strategy, marketing, and finance, to
develop detailed information on the profitability of
Tyco's primary markets as well as the product or service
offerings, costs, and price positioning relative to the
competition. The teams met with corporate executives
biweekly during Breen's first six months to review and
discuss the findings. These discussions focused on the
assumptions that would drive each unit's long-term
financial performance, not on the financial forecasts
themselves. In fact, once assumptions about market
trends were agreed on, it was relatively easy for Tyco's
central finance function to prepare externally oriented
and internally consistent forecasts for each unit.

Separating the process of building assumptions from
that of preparing financial projections helps to ground
the business unit–corporate center dialogue in economic
reality. Units can't hide behind specious details, and corporate center executives can't push for unrealistic goals.
What's more, the fact-based discussion resulting from
this kind of approach builds trust between the top team
and each unit and removes barriers to fast and effective
execution. "When you understand the fundamentals and
performance drivers in a detailed way," says Bob Diamond, "you can then step back, and you don't have to
manage the details. The team knows which issues it can
get on with, which it needs to flag to me, and which
issues we really need to work out together."

*Rule 3: Use a rigorous framework, speak a common
language.* To be productive the dialogue between the

corporate center and the business units about market trends and assumptions must be conducted within a rigorous framework. Many of the companies we advise use the concept of profit pools, which draws on the competition theories of Michael Porter and others. In this framework, a business's long-term financial performance is tied to the total profit pool available in each of the markets it serves and its share of each profit pool—which, in turn, is tied to the business's market share and relative profitability versus competitors in each market.

In this approach, the first step is for the corporate center and the unit team to agree on the size and growth of each profit pool. Fiercely competitive markets, such as pulp and paper or commercial airlines, have small (or negative) total profit pools. Less competitive markets, like soft drinks or pharmaceuticals, have large total profit pools. We find it helpful to estimate the size of each profit pool directly—through detailed benchmarking—and then forecast changes in the pool's size and growth. Each business unit then assesses what share of the total profit pool it can realistically capture over time, given its business model and positioning. Competitively advantaged businesses can capture a large share of the profit pool—by gaining or sustaining a high market share, generating above-average profitability, or both. Competitively disadvantaged businesses, by contrast, typically capture a negligible share of the profit pool. Once the unit and the corporate center agree on the likely share of the pool the business will capture over time, the corporate center can easily create the financial projections that will serve as the unit's road map.

In our view, the specific framework a company uses to ground its strategic plans isn't all that important. What is critical is that the framework establish a common language for the dialogue between the corporate center and the units—one that the strategy, marketing, and finance teams all understand and use. Without a rigorous framework to link a business's performance in the product markets with its financial performance over time, it is very difficult for top management to ascertain whether the financial projections that accompany a business unit's strategic plan are reasonable and realistically achievable. As a result, management can't know with confidence whether a performance shortfall stems from poor execution or an unrealistic and ungrounded plan.

Rule 4: Discuss resource deployments early. Companies can create more realistic forecasts and more executable plans if they discuss up front the level and timing of critical resource deployments. At Cisco Systems, for example, a cross-functional team reviews the level and timing of resource deployments early in the planning stage. These teams regularly meet with John Chambers (CEO), Dennis Powell (CFO), Randy Pond (VP of operations), and the other members of Cisco's executive team to discuss their findings and make recommendations. Once agreement is reached on resource allocation and timing at the unit level, those elements are factored into the company's two-year plan. Cisco then monitors each unit's actual resource deployments on a monthly basis (as well as its performance) to make sure things are going according to plan and that the plan is generating the expected results.

Challenging business units about when new resources need to be in place focuses the planning dialogue on what actually needs to happen across the company in order to execute each unit's strategy. Critical questions invariably surface, such as: How long will it take us to change customers' purchase patterns? How fast can we deploy our new sales force? How quickly will competitors respond? These are tough questions. But answering them makes the forecasts and the plans they accompany more feasible.

What's more, an early assessment of resource needs also informs discussions about market trends and drivers, improving the quality of the strategic plan and making it far more executable. In the course of talking about the resources needed to expand in the rapidly growing cable market, for example, Cisco came to realize that additional growth would require more trained engineers to improve existing products and develop new features. So, rather than relying on the functions to provide these resources from the bottom up, corporate management earmarked a specific number of trained engineers to support growth in cable. Cisco's financial-planning organization carefully monitors the engineering head count, the pace of feature development, and revenues generated by the business to make sure the strategy stays on track.

Rule 5: Clearly identify priorities. To deliver any strategy successfully, managers must make thousands of tactical decisions and put them into action. But not all tactics are equally important. In most instances, a few key steps must be taken—at the right time and in the right way—to meet planned performance. Leading companies make these priorities explicit so that each executive has a clear sense of where to direct his or her efforts.

At Textron, a $10 billion multi-industrial conglomerate, each business unit identifies "improvement priorities" that it must act upon to realize the performance outlined in its strategic plan. Each improvement priority is translated into action items with clearly defined accountabilities, timetables, and key performance indicators (KPIs) that allow executives to tell how a unit is delivering on a priority. Improvement priorities and action items cascade to every level at the company—from the management committee (consisting of Textron's top five executives) down to the lowest levels in each of the company's ten business units. Lewis Campbell, Textron's CEO, summarizes the company's approach this way: "Everyone needs to know: 'If I have only one hour to work, here's what I'm going to focus on.' Our goal deployment process makes each individual's accountabilities and priorities clear."

The Swiss pharmaceutical giant Roche goes as far as to turn its business plans into detailed performance contracts that clearly specify the steps needed and the risks that must be managed to achieve the plans. These contracts all include a "delivery agenda" that lists the five to ten critical priorities with the greatest impact on performance. By maintaining a delivery agenda at each level of the company, Chairman and CEO Franz Humer and his leadership team make sure "everyone at Roche understands exactly what we have agreed to do at a strategic level and that our strategy gets translated into clear execution priorities. Our delivery agenda helps us stay the course with the strategy decisions we have made so that execution is actually allowed to happen. We cannot control implementation from HQ, but we can agree on the priorities, communicate relentlessly, and hold managers accountable for executing against their commitments."

Rule 6: Continuously monitor performance. Seasoned executives know almost instinctively whether a business has asked for too much, too little, or just enough resources to deliver the goods. They develop this capability over time—essentially through trial and error. High-performing companies use real-time performance tracking to help accelerate this trial-and-error process. They continuously monitor their resource deployment patterns and their results against plan, using continuous feedback to reset planning assumptions and reallocate resources. This real-time information allows management to spot and remedy flaws in the plan and shortfalls in execution—and to avoid confusing one with the other.

At Textron, for example, each KPI is carefully monitored, and regular operating reviews percolate performance shortfalls—or "red light" events—up through the management ranks. This provides CEO Lewis Campbell, CFO Ted French, and the other members of Textron's management committee with the information they need to spot and fix breakdowns in execution.

A similar approach has played an important role in the dramatic revival of Dow Chemical's fortunes. In December 2001, with performance in a free fall, Dow's board of directors asked Bill Stavropoulos (Dow's CEO from 1993 to 1999) to return to the helm. Stavropoulos and Andrew Liveris (the current CEO, then COO) immediately focused Dow's entire top leadership team on execution through a project they called the Performance Improvement Drive. They began by defining clear performance metrics for each of Dow's 79 business units. Performance on these key metrics was tracked against plans on a weekly basis, and the entire leadership team discussed any serious discrepancies first thing every Monday morning. As Liveris told us, the weekly monitoring sessions "forced everyone to live the details of execution" and let "the entire organization know how we were performing."

Continuous monitoring of performance is particularly important in highly volatile industries, where events outside anyone's control can render a plan irrelevant. Under CEO Alan Mulally, Boeing Commercial Airplanes' leadership team holds weekly business performance reviews to track the division's results against its multi-year plan. By tracking the deployment of resources as a leading indicator of whether a plan is being executed effectively, BCA's leadership team can make course corrections each week rather than waiting for quarterly results to roll in.

Furthermore, by proactively monitoring the primary drivers of performance (such as passenger traffic patterns, airline yields and load factors, and new aircraft orders), BCA is better able to develop and deploy effective countermeasures when events throw its plans off course. During the SARS epidemic in late 2002, for example, BCA's leadership team took action to mitigate the adverse consequences of the illness on the business's operating plan within a week of the initial outbreak. The abrupt decline in air traffic to Hong Kong, Singapore, and other Asian business centers signaled that the number of future aircraft deliveries to the region would fall—perhaps precipitously. Accordingly, BCA scaled back its medium-term production plans (delaying the scheduled ramp-up of some programs and accelerating the shutdown of others) and adjusted its multiyear operating plan to reflect the anticipated financial impact.

Rule 7: Reward and develop execution capabilities. No list of rules on this topic would be complete without a reminder that companies have to motivate and develop their staffs; at the end of the day, no process can be better than the people who have to make it work. Unsurprisingly, therefore, nearly all of the companies we studied insisted that the selection and development of management was an essential ingredient in their success. And while improving the capabilities of a company's workforce is no easy task—often taking many years—these capabilities, once built, can drive superior planning and execution for decades.

For Barclays' Bob Diamond, nothing is more important than "ensuring that [the company] hires only A players." In his view, "the hidden costs of bad hiring decisions are enormous, so despite the fact that we are doubling in size, we insist that as a top team we take responsibility for all hiring. The jury of your peers is the toughest judgment, so we vet each others' potential hires and challenge each other to keep raising the bar." It's equally important to make sure that talented hires are rewarded for superior execution. To reinforce its core values of "client," "meritocracy," "team," and "integrity," Barclays Capital has innovative pay schemes that "ring fence" rewards. Stars don't lose out just because the business is entering new markets with lower returns during the growth phase. Says Diamond: "It's so bad for the culture if you don't deliver what you promised to people who have delivered. . . . You've got to make sure you are consistent and fair, unless you want to lose your most productive people."

Companies that are strong on execution also emphasize development. Soon after he became CEO of 3M, Jim McNerney and his top team spent 18 months hashing out a new leadership model for the company. Challenging debates among members of the top team led to agreement on six "leadership attributes"—namely, the ability to "chart the course," "energize and inspire others," "demonstrate ethics, integrity, and compliance," "deliver results," "raise the bar," and "innovate resourcefully." 3M's leadership agreed that these six attributes were essential for the company to become skilled at execution and known for accountability. Today, the leaders credit this model with helping 3M to sustain and even improve its consistently strong performance.

T HE PRIZE FOR CLOSING the strategy-to-
performance gap is huge—an increase in performance of anywhere from 60% to 100% for most companies. But this almost certainly understates the true
benefits. Companies that create tight links between their
strategies, their plans, and, ultimately, their performance
often experience a cultural multiplier effect. Over time,
as they turn their strategies into great performance, leaders in these organizations become much more confident
in their own capabilities and much more willing to make
the stretch commitments that inspire and transform
large companies. In turn, individual managers who keep
their commitments are rewarded—with faster progres-
sion and fatter paychecks—reinforcing the behaviors
needed to drive any company forward.

Eventually, a culture of overperformance emerges. Investors start giving management the benefit of the doubt
when it comes to bold moves and performance delivery.
The result is a performance premium on the company's
stock—one that further rewards stretch commitments
and performance delivery. Before long, the company's
reputation among potential recruits rises, and a virtuous
circle is created in which talent begets performance, performance begets rewards, and rewards beget even more
talent. In short, closing the strategy-to-performance gap
is not only a source of immediate performance improvement but also an important driver of cultural change with
a large and lasting impact on the organization's capabilities, strategies, and competitiveness.

Originally published in July–August 2005
Reprint R0507E

Moments of Greatness

*Entering the Fundamental
State of Leadership*

ROBERT E. QUINN

Executive Summary

WHEN WE DO OUR BEST WORK as leaders, we don't imitate others. Rather, we draw on our own values and capabilities. We enter what author Robert Quinn calls the *fundamental state of leadership*. This is a frame of mind we tend to adopt when facing a significant challenge: a promotion opportunity, the risk of professional failure, a serious illness, a divorce, the death of a loved one, or any other major life jolt. Crisis calls, and we rise to the occasion.

But we don't need to spend time in the dark night of the soul to reach this fundamental state. We can make the shift at any time by asking ourselves—and honestly answering—four transformative questions:

Am I results centered? (Am I willing to leave my comfort zone to make things happen?)

Am I internally directed? (Am I behaving according to my values rather than bending to social or political pressures?)

Am I other focused? (Am I putting the collective good above my own needs?)

Am I externally open? (Am I receptive to outside stimuli that may signal the need for change?)

When we can answer these questions in the affirmative, we're prepared to lead in the truest sense.

Of course, we can't sustain the fundamental state of leadership indefinitely. Fatigue and external resistance pull us out of it. But each time we reach it, we then return to our everyday selves a bit more capable, and we usually boost the performance of the people around us. Over time, we create a high-performance culture—and that *can* be sustained.

As LEADERS, sometimes we're truly "on," and sometimes we're not. Why is that? What separates the episodes of excellence from those of mere competence? In striving to tip the balance toward excellence, we try to identify great leaders' qualities and behaviors so we can develop them ourselves. Nearly all corporate training programs and books on leadership are grounded in the assumption that we should study the behaviors of those who have been successful and teach people to emulate them.

But my colleagues and I have found that when leaders do their best work, they don't copy anyone. Instead, they draw on their own fundamental values and capabilities—operating in a frame of mind that is true to them yet, paradoxically, not their normal state of being. I call it the *fundamental state of leadership*. It's the way we lead

when we encounter a crisis and finally choose to move
forward. Think back to a time when you faced a significant life challenge: a promotion opportunity, the risk of
professional failure, a serious illness, a divorce, the death
of a loved one, or any other major jolt. Most likely, if you
made decisions not to meet others' expectations but to
suit what you instinctively understood to be right—in
other words, if you were at your very best—you rose to
the task because you were being tested.

Is it possible to enter the fundamental state of leadership without crisis? In my work coaching business executives, I've found that if we ask ourselves—and honestly
answer—just four questions, we can make the shift at
any time. It's a temporary state. Fatigue and external
resistance pull us out of it. But each time we reach it, we
return to our everyday selves a bit more capable, and
we usually elevate the performance of the people around
us as well. Over time, we all can become more effective
leaders by deliberately choosing to enter the fundamental state of leadership rather than waiting for crisis to
force us there.

Defining the Fundamental State

Even those who are widely admired for their seemingly
easy and natural leadership skills—presidents, prime
ministers, CEOs—do not usually function in the fundamental state of leadership. Most of the time, they are in
their normal state—a healthy and even necessary condition under many circumstances, but not one that's con-
ducive to coping with crisis. In the normal state, people
tend to stay within their comfort zones and allow external forces to direct their behaviors and decisions. They
lose moral influence and often rely on rational argument

and the exercise of authority to bring about change. Others comply with what these leaders ask, out of fear, but the result is usually unimaginative and incremental—and largely reproduces what already exists.

To elevate the performance of others, we must elevate ourselves into the fundamental state of leadership. Getting there requires a shift along four dimensions. (See the exhibit "There's Normal, and There's Fundamental.")

First, we move from being comfort centered to being results centered. The former feels safe but eventually leads to a sense of languishing and meaninglessness. In

---

There's Normal, and There's Fundamental

Under everyday circumstances, leaders can remain in their normal state of being and do what they need to do. But some challenges require a heightened perspective—what can be called the fundamental state of leadership. Here's how the two states differ.

In the normal state, I am . . .	In the fundamental state, I am . . .
Comfort centered	Results centered
I stick with what I know.	I venture beyond familiar territory to pursue ambitious new outcomes.
Externally directed	Internally directed
I comply with others' wishes in an effort to keep the peace.	I behave according to my values.
Self-focused	Other focused
I place my interests above those of the group.	I put the collective good first.
Internally closed	Internally open
I block out external stimuli in order to stay on task and avoid risk.	I learn from my environment and recognize when there's a need for change.

his book *The Path of Least Resistance,* Robert Fritz carefully explains how asking a single question can move us from the normal, reactive state to a much more generative condition. That question is this: What result do I want to create? Giving an honest answer pushes us off nature's path of least resistance. It leads us from problem solving to purpose finding.

Second, we move from being externally directed to being more internally directed. That means that we stop merely complying with others' expectations and conforming to the current culture. To become more internally directed is to clarify our core values and increase our integrity, confidence, and authenticity. As we become more confident and more authentic, we behave differently. Others must make sense of our new behavior. Some will be attracted to it, and some will be offended by it. That's not prohibitive, though: When we are true to our values, we are willing to initiate such conflict.

Third, we become less self-focused and more focused on others. We put the needs of the organization as a whole above our own. Few among us would admit that personal needs trump the collective good, but the impulse to control relationships in a way that feeds our own interests is natural and normal. That said, self-focus over time leads to feelings of isolation. When we put the collective good first, others reward us with their trust and respect. We form tighter, more sensitive bonds. Empathy increases, and cohesion follows. We create an enriched sense of community, and that helps us transcend the conflicts that are a necessary element in high-performing organizations.

Fourth, we become more open to outside signals or stimuli, including those that require us to do things we are not comfortable doing. In the normal state, we pay attention to signals that we know to be relevant. If they suggest incremental adjustments, we respond. If, however, they call for more dramatic changes, we may adopt a posture of defensiveness and denial; this mode of self-protection and self-deception separates us from the ever-changing external world. We live according to an outdated, less valid, image of what is real. But in the fundamental state of leadership, we are more aware of what is unfolding, and we generate new images all the time. We are adaptive, credible, and unique. In this externally open state, no two people are alike.

These four qualities—being results centered, internally directed, other focused, and externally open—are at the heart of positive human influence, which is generative and attractive. A person without these four characteristics can also be highly influential, but his or her influence tends to be predicated on some form of control or force, which does not usually give rise to committed followers. By entering the fundamental state of leadership, we increase the likelihood of attracting others to an elevated level of community, a high-performance state that may continue even when we are not present.

Preparing for the Fundamental State

Because people usually do not leave their comfort zones unless forced, many find it helpful to follow a process when they choose to enter the fundamental state of leadership. I teach a technique to executives and use it in my own work. It simply involves asking four awareness-raising questions designed to help us transcend our natural denial mechanisms. When people become aware of their hypocrisies, they are more likely to change. Those who are new to the "fundamental state" concept, however, need to take two preliminary steps before they can understand and employ it.

Step 1: Recognize that you have previously entered the fundamental state of leadership. Every reader of this publication has reached, at one time or another, the fundamental state of leadership. We've all faced a great personal or professional challenge and spent time in the dark night of the soul. In successfully working through such episodes, we inevitably enter the fundamental state of leadership.

When I introduce people to this concept, I ask them to identify two demanding experiences from their past and ponder what happened in terms of intention, integrity, trust, and adaptability. At first, they resist the exercise because I am asking them to revisit times of great personal pain. But as they recount their experiences, they begin to see that they are also returning to moments of greatness. Our painful experiences often bring out our best selves. Recalling the lessons of such moments releases positive emotions and makes it easier to see what's possible in the present. In this exercise, I ask people to consider their behavior during these episodes in relation to the characteristics of the fundamental state of leadership. (See the exhibit "You've Already Been There" for analyses of two actual episodes.)

Sometimes I also ask workshop participants to share their stories with one another. Naturally, they are reluctant to talk about such dark moments. To help people open up, I share my own moments of great challenge, the ones I would normally keep to myself. By exhibiting vulnerability, I'm able to win the group's trust and embolden other people to exercise the same courage. I recently ran a workshop with a cynical group of executives. After I broke

You've Already Been There

Two participants in a leadership workshop at the University of Michigan's Ross School of Business used this self-assessment tool to figure out how they've transcended their greatest life challenges by entering the fundamental state of leadership. You can use the same approach in analyzing how you've conquered your most significant challenges.

	Participant A	Participant B
The pivotal crisis:	I was thrust into a job that was crucial to the organization but greatly exceeded my capabilities. I had to get people to do things they did not want to do.	I was driving myself hard at work, and things kept getting worse at home. Finally my wife told me she wanted a divorce.
How did you become more results centered?	I kept trying to escape doing what was required, but I could not stand the guilt. I finally decided I had to change. I envisioned what success might look like, and I committed to making whatever changes were necessary.	I felt I'd lost everything: family, wealth, and stature. I withdrew from relationships. I started drinking heavily. I finally sought professional help for my sorrow and, with guidance, clarified my values and made choices about my future.

How did you become more internally directed?	I stopped worrying so much about how other people would evaluate and judge me. I was starting to operate from my own values. I felt more self-empowered than ever and realized how fear driven I had been.	I engaged in a lot of self-reflection and journal writing. It became clear that I was not defined by marriage, wealth, or stature. I was more than that. I began to focus on how I could make a difference for other people. I got more involved in my community.
How did you become more focused on others?	I realized how much I needed people, and I became more concerned about them. I was better able to hear what they were saying. I talked not just from my head but also from my heart. My colleagues responded. Today, I am still close to those people.	As I started to grow and feel more self-confident, I became better at relating. At work, I now ask more of people than I ever did before, but I also give them far more support. I care about them, and they can tell.
How did you become more externally open?	I experimented with new approaches. They often did not work, but they kept the brain-storming in motion. I paid attention to every kind of feedback. I was hungry to get it right. There was a lot of discovery. Each step forward was exhilarating.	I began to feel stronger. I was less intimidated when people gave me negative feedback. I think it was because I was less afraid of changing and growing.

the testimonial ice, one of the participants told us of a time when he had accepted a new job that required him to relocate his family. Just before he was to start, his new boss called in a panic, asking him to cut his vacation short and begin work immediately. The entire New England engineering team had quit; clients in the region had no support whatsoever. The executive started his job early, and his family had to navigate the move without his help. He described the next few months as "the worst and best experience" of his life.

Another executive shared that he'd found out he had cancer the same week he was promoted and relocated to Paris, not knowing how to speak French. His voice cracked as he recalled these stressful events. But then he told us about the good that came out of them—how he conquered both the disease and the job while also becoming a more authentic and influential leader.

Others came forward with their own stories, and I saw a great change in the group. The initial resistance and cynicism began to disappear, and participants started exploring the fundamental state of leadership in a serious way. They saw the power in the concept and recognized that hiding behind their pride or reputation would only get in the way of future progress. In recounting their experiences, they came to realize that they had become more purposive, authentic, compassionate, and responsive.

Step 2: Analyze your current state.   When we're in the fundamental state, we take on various positive characteristics, such as clarity of vision, self-empowerment, empathy, and creative thinking. (See the exhibit "Are You in the Fundamental State of Leadership?" for a checklist organized along the four dimensions.) Most of

Are You in the Fundamental State of Leadership?

Think of a time when you reached the fundamental state of leadership—that is, when you were at your best as a leader—and use this checklist to identify the qualities you displayed. Then check off the items that describe your behavior today. Compare the past and present. If there's a significant difference, what changes do you need to make to get back to the fundamental state?

**At my best
I was . . .**   **Today I
am . . .**

		Results centered
___	___	Knowing what results I'd like to create
___	___	Holding high standards
___	___	Initiating actions
___	___	Challenging people
___	___	Disrupting the status quo
___	___	Capturing people's attention
___	___	Feeling a sense of shared purpose
___	___	Engaging in urgent conversations
		Internally directed
___	___	Operating from my core values
___	___	Finding motivation from within
___	___	Feeling self-empowered
___	___	Leading courageously
___	___	Bringing hidden conflicts to the surface
___	___	Expressing what I really believe
___	___	Feeling a sense of shared reality
___	___	Engaging in authentic conversations
		Other focused
___	___	Sacrificing personal interests for the common good
___	___	Seeing the potential in everyone
___	___	Trusting others and fostering interdependence
___	___	Empathizing with people's needs
___	___	Expressing concern
___	___	Supporting people
___	___	Feeling a sense of shared identity
___	___	Engaging in participative conversations
		Externally open
___	___	Moving forward into uncertainty
___	___	Inviting feedback
___	___	Paying deep attention to what's unfolding
___	___	Learning exponentially
___	___	Watching for new opportunities
___	___	Growing continually
___	___	Feeling a sense of shared contribution
___	___	Engaging in creative conversations

us would like to say we display these characteristics at all times, but we really do so only sporadically.

Comparing our normal performance with what we have done at our very best often creates a desire to elevate what we are doing now. Knowing we've operated at a higher level in the past instills confidence that we can do so again; it quells our fear of stepping into unknown and risky territory.

Asking Four Transformative Questions

Of course, understanding the fundamental state of leadership and recognizing its power are not the same as being there. Entering that state is where the real work comes in. To get started, we can ask ourselves four questions that correspond with the four qualities of the fundamental state.

To show how each of these qualities affects our behavior while we're in the fundamental state of leadership, I'll draw on stories from two executives. One is a company president; we'll call him John Jones. The other, Robert Yamamoto, is the executive director of the Los Angeles Junior Chamber of Commerce. Both once struggled with major challenges that changed the way they thought about their jobs and their lives.

I met John in an executive course I was teaching. He was a successful change leader who had turned around two companies in his corporation. Yet he was frustrated. He had been promised he'd become president of the largest company in the corporation as soon as the current president retired, which would happen in the near future. In the meantime, he had been told to bide his time with a company that everyone considered dead. His assignment was simply to oversee the funeral, yet he took it as a personal challenge to turn the company around. After he had been there nine months, however, there was little improvement, and the people were still not very engaged.

As for Robert, he had been getting what he considered to be acceptable (if not exceptional) results in his company. So when the new board president asked him to prepare a letter of resignation, Robert was stunned. He underwent a period of anguished introspection, during which he began to distrust others and question his own management skills and leadership ability. Concerned for his family and his future, he started to seek another job and wrote the requested letter.

As you will see, however, even though things looked grim for both Robert and John, they were on the threshold of positive change.

AM I RESULTS CENTERED?

Most of the time, we are comfort centered. We try to continue doing what we know how to do. We may think we are pursuing new outcomes, but if achieving them means leaving our comfort zones, we subtly—even unconsciously—find ways to avoid doing so. We typically advocate ambitious outcomes while designing our work for maximum administrative convenience, which allows us to avoid conflict but frequently ends up reproducing what already exists. Often, others collude with us to act out this deception. Being comfort centered is hypocritical, self-deceptive, and normal.

Clarifying the result we want to create requires us to reorganize our lives. Instead of moving away from a problem, we move toward a possibility that does not yet exist. We become more proactive, intentional, optimistic, invested, and persistent. We also tend to become more energized, and our impact on others becomes energizing.

Consider what happened with John. When I first spoke with him, he sketched out his strategy with little enthusiasm. Sensing that lack of passion, I asked him a question designed to test his commitment to the end he claimed he wanted to obtain:

> *What if you told your people the truth? Suppose you told them that nobody really expects you to succeed, that you were assigned to be a caretaker for 18 months, and that you have been promised a plum job once your assignment is through. And then you tell them that you have chosen instead to give up that plum job and bet your career on the people present. Then, from your newly acquired stance of optimism for the company's prospects, you issue some challenges beyond your employees' normal capacity.*

To my surprise, John responded that he was beginning to think along similar lines. He grabbed a napkin and rapidly sketched out a new strategy along with a plan for carrying it out, including reassignments for his staff. It was clear and compelling, and he was suddenly full of energy.

What happened here? John was the president of his company and therefore had authority. And he'd turned around two other companies—evidence that he had the knowledge and competencies of a change leader. Yet he was *failing* as a change leader. That's because he had slipped into his comfort zone. He was going through the motions, doing what had worked elsewhere. He was imitating a great leader—in this case, John himself. But imitation is not the way to enter the fundamental state of leadership. If I had accused John of not being committed to a real vision, he would have been incensed. He would have argued heatedly in denial of the truth. All I had to do, though, was nudge him in the right direction. As soon as he envisioned the result he wanted to create and committed himself to it, a new strategy emerged and he was reenergized.

Then there was Robert, who went to what he assumed would be his last board meeting and found that he had more support than he'd been led to believe. Shockingly, at the end of the meeting, he still had his job. Even so, this fortuitous turn brought on further soul-searching. Robert started to pay more attention to what he was doing; he began to see his tendency to be tactical and to gravitate toward routine tasks. He concluded that he was managing, not leading. He was playing a role and abdicating leadership to the board president—not because that person had the knowledge and vision to lead but because the position came with the statutory right to lead. "I suddenly decided to really lead my organization," Robert said. "It was as if a new person emerged. The decision was not about me. I needed to do it for the good of the organization."

In deciding to "really lead," Robert started identifying the strategic outcomes he wanted to create. As he did this, he found himself leaving his zone of comfort— behaving in new ways and generating new outcomes.

AM I INTERNALLY DIRECTED?

In the normal state, we comply with social pressures in order to avoid conflict and remain connected with our coworkers. However, we end up feeling *less* connected because conflict avoidance results in political compromise. We begin to lose our uniqueness and our sense of integrity. The agenda gradually shifts from creating an external result to preserving political peace. As this problem intensifies, we begin to lose hope and energy.

This loss was readily apparent in the case of John. He was his corporation's shining star. But since he was at least partially focused on the future reward—the plum job—he was not fully focused on doing the hard work he needed to do at the moment. So he didn't ask enough of the people he was leading. To get more from them, John needed to be more internally directed.

AM I OTHER FOCUSED?

It's hard to admit, but most of us, most of the time, put our own needs above those of the whole. Indeed, it is healthy to do so; it's a survival mechanism. But when the pursuit of our own interests controls our relationships, we erode others' trust in us. Although people may comply with our wishes, they no longer derive energy from their relationships with us. Over time we drive away the very social support we seek.

To become more focused on others is to commit to the collective good in relationships, groups, or organizations, even if it means incurring personal costs. When John made the shift into the fundamental state of leadership, he committed to an uncertain future for himself. He had been promised a coveted job. All he had to do was wait a few months. Still, he was unhappy, so he chose to turn down the opportunity in favor of a course that was truer to his leadership values. When he shifted gears, he sacrificed his personal security in favor of a greater good.

Remember Robert's words: "The decision was not about me. I needed to do it for the good of the organization." After entering the fundamental state of leadership, he proposed a new strategic direction to the board's president and said that if the board didn't like it, he would walk away with no regrets. He knew that the strategy would benefit the organization, regardless of how it would affect him personally. Robert put the good of the organization first. When a leader does this, people notice, and the leader gains respect and trust. Group members, in turn, become more likely to put the collective good first. When they do, tasks that previously seemed impossible become doable.

AM I EXTERNALLY OPEN?

Being closed to external stimuli has the benefit of keeping us on task, but it also allows us to ignore signals that suggest a need for change. Such signals would force us to cede control and face risk, so denying them is self-protective, but it is also self-deceptive. John convinced himself he'd done all he could for his failing company when, deep down, he knew that he had the capacity to improve things. Robert was self-deceptive, too, until crisis and renewed opportunity caused him to open up and explore the fact that he was playing a role accorded him but not using his knowledge and emotional capacity to transcend that role and truly lead his people.

Asking ourselves whether we're externally open shifts our focus from controlling our environment to learning from it and helps us recognize the need for change. Two things happen as a result. First, we are forced to improvise in response to previously unrecognized cues—that is, to depart from established routines. And second, because trial-and-error survival requires an accurate picture of the results we're creating, we actively and genuinely seek honest feedback. Since people trust us more when we're in this state, they tend to offer more accurate feedback, understanding that we are likely to learn from the message rather than kill the messenger. A cycle of learning and empowerment is created, allowing us to see things that people normally cannot see and to formulate transformational strategies.

Applying the Fundamental Principles

Just as I teach others about the fundamental state of leadership, I also try to apply the concept in my own life. I was a team leader on a project for the University of Michigan's Executive Education Center. Usually, the center runs weeklong courses that bring in 30 to 40 executives. It was proposed that we develop a new product, an integrated week of perspectives on leadership. C.K. Prahalad would begin with a strategic perspective, then Noel Tichy, Dave Ulrich, Karl Weick, and I would follow with our own presentations. The objective was to fill a 400-seat auditorium. Since each presenter had a reasonably large following in some domain of the executive world, we were confident we could fill the seats, so we scheduled the program for the month of July, when our facilities were typically underutilized.

In the early months of planning and organizing, everything went perfectly. A marketing consultant had said we could expect to secure half our enrollment three weeks prior to the event. When that time rolled around, slightly less than half of the target audience had signed up, so we thought all was well. But then a different consultant indicated that for our kind of event we would get few additional enrollments during the last three weeks. This stunning prediction meant that attendance would be half of what we expected and we would be lucky to break even.

As the team leader, I could envision the fallout. Our faculty members, accustomed to drawing a full house, would be offended by a half-empty room; the dean would want to know what went wrong; and the center's staff would probably point to the team leader as the problem. That night I spent several hours pacing the floor. I was filled with dread and shame. Finally I told myself that this kind of behavior was useless. I went to my desk and wrote down the four questions. As I considered them, I concluded that I was comfort centered, externally directed, self-focused, and internally closed.

So I asked myself, "What result do I want to create?" I wrote that I wanted the center to learn how to offer a new, world-class product that would be in demand over time. With that clarification came a freeing insight: Because this was our first offering of the product, turning a large profit was not essential. That would be nice, of course, but we'd be happy to learn how to do such an event properly, break even, and lay the groundwork for making a profit in the future.

I then asked myself, "How can I become other focused?" At that moment, I was totally self-focused—I was worried about my reputation—and my first inclination was to be angry with the staff. But in shifting my focus to what they might be thinking that night, I realized they were most likely worried that I'd come to work in the morning ready to assign blame. Suddenly, I saw a need to both challenge and support them.

Finally, I thought about how I could become externally open. It would mean moving forward and learning something new, even if that made me uncomfortable. I needed to engage in an exploratory dialogue rather than preside as the expert in charge.

I immediately began making a list of marketing strategies, though I expected many of them would prove foolish since I knew nothing about marketing. The next day, I brought the staff together—and they, naturally, were guarded. I asked them what result we wanted to create. What happened next is a good example of how contagious the fundamental state of leadership can be.

We talked about strategies for increasing attendance, and after a while, I told the staff that I had some silly marketing ideas and was embarrassed to share them but was willing to do anything to help. They laughed at many of my naive thoughts about how to increase publicity and create pricing incentives. Yet my proposals also sparked serious discussion, and the group began to brainstorm its way into a collective strategy. Because I was externally open, there was space and time for everyone to lead. People came up with better ways of approaching media outlets and creating incentives. In that meeting, the group developed a shared sense of purpose, reality, identity, and contribution. They left feeling reasonable optimism and went forward as a committed team.

In the end, we did not get 400 participants, but we filled more than enough seats to have a successful event. We more than broke even, and we developed the skills we needed to run such an event better in the future. The program was a success because something transformational occurred among the staff. Yet the transformation did not originate in the meeting. It began the night before, when I asked myself the four questions and moved from the normal, reactive state to the fundamental state of leadership. And my entry into the fundamental state encouraged the staff to enter as well.

While the fundamental state proves useful in times of crisis, it can also help us cope with more mundane challenges. If I am going to have an important conversation, attend a key meeting, participate in a significant event, or teach a class, part of my preparation is to try to reach the fundamental state of leadership. Whether I am working with an individual, a group, or an organization, I ask the same four questions. They often lead to high-performance outcomes, and the repetition of high-performance outcomes can eventually create a high-performance culture.

Inspiring Others to High Performance

When we enter the fundamental state of leadership, we immediately have new thoughts and engage in new behaviors. We can't remain in this state forever. It can last for hours, days, or sometimes months, but eventually we come back to our normal frame of mind. While the fundamental state is temporary, each time we are in it we learn more about people and our environment and increase the probability that we will be able to return to it. Moreover, we inspire those around us to higher levels of performance.

To this day, Robert marvels at the contrast between his organization's past and present. His transformation into a leader with positive energy and a willingness and ability to tackle challenges in new ways helped shape the L.A. Junior Chamber of Commerce into a high-functioning and creative enterprise. When I last spoke to Robert, here's what he had to say:

> *I have a critical mass of individuals on both the staff and the board who are willing to look at our challenges in a new way and work on solutions together. At our meetings, new energy is present. What previously seemed unimaginable now seems to happen with ease.*

Any CEO would be delighted to be able to say these things. But the truth is, it's not a typical situation. When Robert shifted into the fundamental state of leadership, his group (which started off in a normal state) came to life, infused with his renewed energy and vision. Even after he'd left the fundamental state, the group sustained a higher level of performance. It continues to flourish, without significant staff changes or restructuring.

All this didn't happen because Robert read a book or an article about the best practices of some great leader. It did not happen because he was imitating someone else. It happened because he was jolted out of his comfort zone and was forced to enter the fundamental state of leadership. He was driven to clarify the result he wanted to create, to act courageously from his core values, to surrender his self-interest to the collective good, and to open himself up to learning in real time. From Robert, and others like him, we can learn the value of challenging ourselves in this way—a painful process but one with great potential to make a positive impact on our own lives and on the people around us.

Originally published in July–August 2005
Reprint R0507F

Learning in the Thick of It

MARILYN DARLING, CHARLES PARRY,
AND JOSEPH MOORE

Executive Summary

THE U.S. ARMY'S OPPOSING FORCE (OPFOR) is a
2,500-member brigade whose job is to help prepare
soldiers for combat. Created to be the meanest,
toughest foe that soldiers will ever face, OPFOR engages units-in-training in a variety of mock campaigns
under a wide range of conditions. Every month, a fresh
brigade of more than 4,000 soldiers takes on this
standing enemy.

OPFOR, which is stationed in the California desert,
always has the home-court advantage. But the force
being trained—called BLUFOR—is numerically and technologically superior. It possesses more resources and
better, more available data. It is made up of experienced soldiers. And it knows just what to expect,
because OPFOR shares its methods from previous campaigns with BLUFOR's commanders. In short, each

BLUFOR brigade is given practically every edge. Yet OPFOR almost always wins.

Underlying OPFOR's consistent success is the way it uses the after-action review (AAR), a method for extracting lessons from one event or project and applying them to others. AAR meetings became a popular business tool after Shell Oil began experimenting with them in 1998. Most corporate AARs, however, are faint echoes of the rigorous reviews performed by OPFOR. Companies tend to treat the process as a pro-forma wrap-up, drawing lessons from an action but rarely learning them. OPFOR's AARs, by contrast, generate raw material that is fed back into the execution cycle. And while OPFOR's reviews extract numerous lessons, the brigade does not consider a lesson to be learned until it is successfully applied and validated.

It might not make sense for companies to adopt OPFOR's AAR processes in their entirety, but four fundamentals are mandatory: Lessons must benefit the team that extracts them. The AAR process must start at the beginning of the activity. Lessons must link explicitly to future actions. And leaders must hold everyone, especially themselves, accountable for learning.

IMAGINE AN ORGANIZATION that confronts constantly changing competitors. That is always smaller and less well-equipped than its opponents. That routinely cuts its manpower and resources. That turns over a third of its leaders every year. And that still manages to win competition after competition after competition.

The U.S. Army's Opposing Force (commonly known as OPFOR), a 2,500-member brigade whose job is to help prepare soldiers for combat, is just such an organization.

Created to be the meanest, toughest foe troops will ever face, OPFOR engages units-in-training in a variety of mock campaigns under a wide range of conditions. (See "Learning to Be OPFOR" at the end of this article.) Every month, a fresh brigade of more than 4,000 soldiers takes on this standing enemy, which, depending on the scenario, may play the role of a hostile army or insurgents, paramilitary units, or terrorists. The two sides battle on foot, in tanks, and in helicopters dodging artillery, land mines, and chemical weapons.

Stationed on a vast, isolated stretch of California desert, OPFOR has the home-court advantage. But the force that's being trained—called Blue Force, or BLUFOR, for the duration of the exercise—is numerically and technologically superior. It possesses more dedicated resources and better, more rapidly available data. It is made up of experienced soldiers. And it knows just what to expect, because OPFOR shares its methods from previous campaigns with BLUFOR's commanders. In short, each of these very capable BLUFOR brigades is given practically every edge. Yet OPFOR almost always wins.

Underlying OPFOR's consistent success is the way it uses the *after-action review* (AAR), a method for extracting lessons from one event or project and applying them to others. The AAR, which has evolved over the past two decades, originated at OPFOR's parent organization, the National Training Center (NTC). AAR meetings became a popular business tool after Shell Oil began experimenting with them in 1998 at the suggestion of board member Gordon Sullivan, a retired general. Teams at such companies as Colgate-Palmolive, DTE Energy, Harley-Davidson, and J.M. Huber use these reviews to identify both best practices (which they want to spread) and mistakes (which they don't want to repeat).

Most corporate AARs, however, are faint echoes of the rigorous reviews OPFOR performs. It is simply too easy for companies to turn the process into a pro forma wrap-up. All too often, scrapped projects, poor investments, and failed safety measures end up repeating themselves. Efficient shortcuts, smart solutions, and sound strategies don't.

For companies that want to transform their AARs from postmortems of past failure into aids for future success, there is no better teacher than the technique's master practitioner. OPFOR treats every action as an opportunity for learning—about what to do but also, more important, about how to think. Instead of producing static "knowledge assets" to file away in a management report or repository, OPFOR's AARs generate raw material that the brigade feeds back into the execution cycle. And while OPFOR's reviews extract numerous lessons, the group does not consider a lesson to be truly learned until it is successfully applied and validated.

The battlefield of troops, tanks, and tear gas is very different from the battlefield of products, prices, and profits. But companies that adapt OPFOR's principles to their own practices will be able to integrate leadership, learning, and execution to gain rapid and sustained competitive advantage.

Why Companies Don't Learn

An appreciation of what OPFOR does right begins with an understanding of what businesses do wrong. To see why even organizations that focus on learning often repeat mistakes, we analyzed the AAR and similar "lessons learned" processes at more than a dozen corporations, nonprofits, and government agencies. The fun-

damentals are essentially the same at each: Following a
project or event, team members gather to share insights
and identify mistakes and successes. Their conclusions
are expected to flow—by formal or informal channels—
to other teams and eventually coalesce into best practices and global standards.

Mostly though, that doesn't happen. Although the
companies we studied actively look for lessons, few learn
them in a meaningful way. One leader at a large manufacturing company told us about an after-action review
for a failed project that had already broken down twice
before. Having read reports from the earlier attempts'
AARs—which consisted primarily of one-on-one interviews—she realized with horror after several grueling
hours that the team was "discovering" the same mistakes
all over again.

A somewhat different problem cropped up at a telecom company we visited. A team of project managers
there conducted rigorous milestone reviews and wrap-up
AAR meetings on each of its projects, identifying problems and creating technical fixes to avoid them in future
initiatives. But it made no effort to apply what it was
learning to actions and decisions taken on its current
projects. After several months, the team had so over-
whelmed the system with new steps and checks that the
process itself began causing delays. Rather than improving learning and performance, the AARs were reducing
the team's ability to solve its problems.

We also studied a public agency that was running
dozens of similar projects simultaneously. At the end of
each project, team leaders were asked to complete a
lessons-learned questionnaire about the methods they
would or would not use again; what training the team
had needed; how well members communicated; and

whether the planning had been effective. But the projects ran for years, and memory is less reliable than observation. Consequently, the responses of the few leaders who bothered to fill out the forms were often sweepingly positive—and utterly useless.

Those failures and many more like them stem from three common misconceptions about the nature of an AAR: that it is a meeting, that it is a report, or that it is a postmortem. In fact, an AAR should be more verb than noun—a living, pervasive process that explicitly connects past experience with future action. That is the AAR as it was conceived back in 1981 to help Army leaders adapt quickly in the dynamic, unpredictable situations they were sure to face. And that is the AAR as OPFOR practices it every day.

More than a Meeting

Much of the civilian world's confusion over AARs began because management writers focused only on the AAR meeting itself. OPFOR's AARs, by contrast, are part of a cycle that starts before and continues throughout each campaign against BLUFOR. (BLUFOR units conduct AARs as well, but OPFOR has made a fine art of them.) OPFOR's AAR regimen includes brief huddles, extended planning and review sessions, copious note taking by everyone, and the explicit linking of lessons to future actions.

The AAR cycle for each phase of the campaign begins when the senior commander drafts "operational orders." This document consists of four parts: the task (what actions subordinate units must take); the purpose (why the task is important); the commander's intent (what the senior leader is thinking, explained so that subordinates can pursue his goals even if events don't unfold as expected); and the end state (what the desired result is). It might look like this:

Task. "Seize key terrain in the vicinity of Tiefort City . . ."

Purpose. ". . . so that the main effort can safely pass to the north."

Commander's Intent. "I want to find the enemy's strength and place fixing forces there while our assault force maneuvers to his flank to complete the enemy's defeat. The plan calls for that to happen here, but if it doesn't, you leaders have to tell me where the enemy is and which flank is vulnerable."

End State. "In the end, I want our forces in control of the key terrain, with all enemy units defeated or cut off from their supplies."

The commander shares these orders with his subordinate commanders—the leaders in charge of infantry, munitions, intelligence, logistics, artillery, air, engineers, and communications. He then asks each for a "brief back"—a verbal description of the unit's understanding of its mission (to ensure everyone is on the same page) and its role. This step builds accountability: "You said it. I heard it." The brief back subsequently guides these leaders as they work out execution plans with their subordinates.

Later that day, or the next morning, the commander's executive officer (his second in command) plans and conducts a rehearsal, which includes every key participant.

Most rehearsals take place on a scale model of the battle-field, complete with hills sculpted from sand, spray-painted roads, and placards denoting major landmarks. The rehearsal starts with a restatement of the mission and the senior commander's intent, an intelligence update on enemy positions and strength, and a break-down of the battle's projected critical phases. Each time the executive officer calls out a phase, the unit leaders step out onto the terrain model to the position they expect to occupy during that part of the action. They state their groups' tasks and purposes within the larger mis-sion, the techniques they will apply in that phase, and the resources they expect to have available. After some dis-cussion about what tactics the enemy might use and how units will communicate and coordinate in the thick of battle, the executive officer calls out the next phase and the process is repeated.

As a result of this disciplined preparation, the action that follows becomes a learning experiment. Each unit within OPFOR has established a clear understanding of what it intends to do and how it plans to do it and has shared that understanding with all other units. The units have individually and collectively made predic-tions about what will occur, identified challenges that may arise, and built into their plans ways to address those challenges. So when OPFOR acts, it will be exe-cuting a plan but also observing and testing that plan. The early meetings and rehearsals produce a testable hypothesis: "In *this* situation, given *this* mission, if we take *this* action, we will accomplish *that* outcome." OPFOR is thus able to select the crucial lessons it wants to learn from each action and focus soldiers' attention on them in advance.

Such before-action planning helps establish the agenda for after-action meetings. Conversely, the rigor of the AAR meetings improves the care and precision that go into the before-action planning. As one OPFOR leader explained to us: "We live in an environment where we know we will have an AAR, and we will have to say out loud what worked and what didn't. That leads to asking tough questions during the planning phase or rehearsals so that you know you have it as right as you can get it. No subordinate will let the boss waffle on something for long before challenging him to say it clearly because it will only come out later in the AAR. As a consequence, AAR meetings create a very honest and critical environment well before they begin."

The reference to AAR *meetings*—plural—is important. While a corporate team might conduct one AAR meeting at the end of a six-month project, OPFOR holds dozens of AARs at different levels in a single week. Each unit holds an AAR meeting immediately after each significant phase of an action. If time is short, such meetings may be no more than ten-minute huddles around the hood of a Humvee.

It is common for OPFOR's AARs to be facilitated by the unit leader's executive officer. Virtually all formal AAR meetings begin with a reiteration of the house rules, even if everyone present has already heard them a hundred times: Participate. No thin skins. Leave your stripes at the door. Take notes. Focus on our issues, not the issues of those above us. (The participants' commanders hold their own AARs to address issues at their level.) Absolute candor is critical. To promote a sense of safety, senior leaders stay focused on improving performance, not on placing blame, and are the first to acknowledge their own mistakes.

The AAR leader next launches into a comparison of intended and actual results. She repeats the mission, intent, and expected end state; she then describes the actual end state, along with a brief review of events and any metrics relevant to the objective. For example, if the unit had anticipated that equipment maintenance or logistics would be a challenge, what resources (mines, wire, ammo, vehicles) were functioning and available?

The AAR meeting addresses four questions: What were our intended results? What were our actual results? What caused our results? And what will we sustain or improve? For example:

Sustain. "Continual radio commo checks ensured we could talk with everyone. That became important when BLUFOR took a different route and we needed to reposition many of our forces."

Sustain. "We chose good battle positions. That made it easier to identify friends and foes in infantry."

Improve. "When fighting infantry units, we need to keep better track of the situation so we can attack the infantry before they dismount."

Improve. "How we track infantry. We look for trucks, but we need to look for dismounted soldiers and understand how they'll try to deceive us."

One objective of the AAR, of course, is to determine what worked and what didn't, to help OPFOR refine its ability to predict what will work and what won't in the future. How well did the unit assess its challenges? Were there difficulties it hadn't foreseen? Problems that never materialized? Yes, it is important to correct *things;* but it is more important to correct *thinking.* (OPFOR has determined that flawed assumptions are the most common cause of flawed execution.) Technical corrections affect only the problem that is fixed. A thought-process correction—that is to say, learning—affects the unit's ability to plan, adapt, and succeed in future battles.

More than a Report

At most civilian organizations we studied, teams view the AAR chiefly as a tool for capturing lessons and disseminating them to other teams. Companies that treat AARs this way sometimes even translate the acronym as after-action report instead of after-action review, suggesting that the objective is to create a document intended for other audiences. Lacking a personal stake, team members may participate only because they've been told to or out of loyalty to the company. Members don't expect to learn something useful themselves, so usually they don't.

OPFOR's AARs, by contrast, focus on improving a unit's own learning and, as a result, its own performance. A unit may generate a lesson during the AAR process, but by OPFOR's definition, it won't have learned that lesson until its members have changed their behavior in response. Furthermore, soldiers need to see that it actually works. OPFOR's leaders know most lessons that surface during the first go-round are incomplete or plain wrong, representing what the unit thinks should work and not what really does work. They understand that it takes multiple iterations to produce dynamic solutions that will stand up under any conditions.

For example, in one fight against a small, agile infantry unit, OPFOR had to protect a cave complex containing a large store of munitions. BLUFOR's infantry chose the attack route least anticipated by OPFOR's commanders. Because scouts were slow to observe and communicate the change in BLUFOR's movements, OPFOR was unable to prevent an attack that broke through its defense perimeter. OPFOR was forced to hastily reposition its reserve and forward units. Much of its firepower didn't reach the crucial battle or arrived too late to affect the outcome.

OPFOR's unit leaders knew they could extract many different lessons from this situation. "To fight an agile infantry unit, we must locate and attack infantry before soldiers can leave their trucks" was the first and most basic. But they also knew that that insight was not enough to ensure future success. For example, scouts would have to figure out how to choose patrol routes and observation positions so as to quickly and accurately locate BLUFOR's infantry before it breached the defense. Then staffers would need to determine how to use information from observation points to plan effective artillery missions—in the dark, against a moving target. The next challenge would be to test their assumptions to see first, if they could locate and target infantry sooner; and second, what difference that ability would make to them achieving their mission.

OPFOR's need to test theories is another reason the brigade conducts frequent brief AARs instead of one large wrap-up. The sooner a unit identifies targeting infantry as a skill it must develop, the more opportunities it has to try out different assumptions and strategies during a rotation and the less likely those lessons are to grow stale. So units design numerous small experiments—short cycles of "plan, prepare, execute, AAR"—within longer campaigns. That allows them to validate lessons for their own use and to ensure that the lessons they share with other teams are "complete"—meaning they can be applied in a variety of future situations. More important, soldiers see their performance improve as they apply those lessons, which sustains the learning culture.

Not all OPFOR experiments involve correcting what went wrong. Many involve seeing if what went right will continue to go right under different circumstances. So, for example, if OPFOR has validated the techniques it used to complete a mission, it might try the same mission at night or against an enemy armed with cutting-edge surveillance technology. A consulting-firm ad displays Tiger Woods squinting through the rain to complete a shot and the headline: "Conditions change. Results shouldn't." That could be OPFOR's motto.

In fact, rather than writing off extreme situations as onetime exceptions, OPFOR embraces them as learning opportunities. OPFOR's leaders relish facing an unusual enemy or situation because it allows them to build their repertoire. "It's a chance to measure just how good we are, as opposed to how good we think we are," explained one OPFOR commander. Such an attitude might seem antithetical to companies that can't imagine purposely handicapping themselves in any endeavor. But OPFOR knows that the more challenging the game, the stronger and more agile a competitor it will become.

More than a Postmortem

Corporate AARs are often convened around failed projects. The patient is pronounced dead, and everyone weighs in on the mistakes that contributed to his demise. The word "accountability" comes up a lot—generally it means "blame," which participants expend considerable energy trying to avoid. There is a sense of finality to these sessions. The team is putting a bad experience behind it. (See "Five Ways to Put AARs to Work at Work" at the end of this article.)

"Accountability" comes up a lot during OPFOR's AARs as well, but in that context it is forward-looking rather than backward-looking. Units are accountable for learning their own lessons. And OPFOR's leaders are accountable for taking lessons from one situation and applying them to others—for forging explicit links between past experience and future performance.

At the end of an AAR meeting, the senior commander stands and offers his own assessment of the day's major lessons and how they relate to what was learned and validated during earlier actions. He also identifies the two or three lessons he expects will prove most relevant to the next battle or rotation. If the units focus on more than a few lessons at a time, they risk becoming overwhelmed. If they focus on lessons unlikely to be applied until far in the future, soldiers might forget.

At the meeting following the infantry battle described earlier, for example, the senior commander summed up this way: "To me, this set of battles was a good rehearsal for something we'll see writ large in a few weeks. We really do need to take lessons from these fights, realizing that we'll have a far more mobile attack unit. Deception will be an issue. Multiple routes will be an issue. Our job is to figure out common targets. We need to rethink how to track movement. How many scouts do we need in close to the objective area to see soldiers? They will be extremely well-equipped. So one thing I'm challenging everyone to do is to be prepared to discard your norms next month. It's time to sit down and talk with your sergeants about how you fight a unit with a well-trained infantry."

Immediately after the AAR meeting breaks up, commanders gather their units to conduct their own AARs. Each group applies lessons from these AAR meetings to plan its future actions—for example, repositioning scouts to better track infantry movements in the next battle.

OPFOR also makes its lessons available to BLUFOR: The groups' commanders meet before rotations, and OPFOR's commander allows himself to be "captured" by BLUFOR at the conclusion of battles in order to attend its AARs. At those meetings, the OPFOR commander explains his brigade's planning assumptions and tactics and answers his opponents' questions.

Beyond those conferences with BLUFOR, formally spreading lessons to other units for later application—the chief focus of many corporate AARs—is not in OPFOR's job description. The U.S. Army uses formal knowledge systems to capture and disseminate important lessons to large, dispersed audiences, and the National Training Center contributes indirectly to those. (See "Doctrine and Tactics" at the end of this article.) Informal knowledge sharing among peers, however, is very common. OPFOR's leaders, for example, use e-mail and the Internet to stay in touch with leaders on combat duty. The OPFOR team shares freshly hatched insights and tactics with officers in Afghanistan and Iraq; those officers, in turn, describe new and unexpected situations cropping up in real battles. And, of course, OPFOR's leaders don't stay out in the Mojave Desert forever. Every year as part of the Army's regular rotation, one-third move to other units, which they seed with

OPFOR-spawned thinking. Departing leaders leave behind "continuity folders" full of lessons and AAR notes for their successors.

In an environment where conditions change constantly, knowledge is always a work in progress. So creating, collecting, and sharing knowledge are the responsibility of the people who can apply it. Knowledge is not a staff function.

The Corporate Version

It would be impractical for companies to adopt OPFOR's processes in their entirety. Still, many would benefit from making their own after-action reviews more like OPFOR's. The business landscape, after all, is competitive, protean, and often dangerous. An organization that doesn't merely extract lessons from experience but actually learns them can adapt more quickly and effectively than its rivals. And it is less likely to repeat the kinds of errors that gnaw away at stakeholder value.

Most of the practices we've described can be customized for corporate environments. Simpler forms of operational orders and brief backs, for example, can ensure that a project is seen the same way by everyone on the team and that each member understands his or her role in it. A corporate version, called a before-action review (BAR), requires teams to answer four questions before embarking on an important action: What are our intended results and measures? What challenges can we anticipate? What have we or others learned from similar situations? What will make us successful this time? The responses to those questions align the team's objectives and set the stage for an effective AAR meeting following the action. In addition, breaking projects into smaller chunks, bookended by short BAR and AAR meetings conducted in task-focused groups, establishes feedback loops that can help a project team maximize performance and develop a learning culture over time.

Every organization, every team, and every project will likely require different levels of preparation, execution, and review. However, we have distilled some best practices from the few companies we studied that use AARs well. For example, leaders should phase in an AAR regimen, beginning with the most important and complex work their business units perform. Teams should commit to holding short BAR and AAR meetings as they go, keeping things simple at first and developing the process slowly—adding rehearsals, knowledge-sharing activities and systems, richer metrics, and other features dictated by the particular practice.

While companies will differ on the specifics they adopt, four fundamentals of the OPFOR process are mandatory. Lessons must first and foremost benefit the team that extracts them. The AAR process must start at the beginning of the activity. Lessons must link explicitly to future actions. And leaders must hold everyone, especially themselves, accountable for learning.

By creating tight feedback cycles between thinking and action, AARs build an organization's ability to succeed in a variety of conditions. Former BLUFOR brigades that are now deploying to the Middle East take with them not just a set of lessons but also a refresher course on how to draw new lessons from situations for which they did not train—situations they may not even have imagined. In a fast-changing environment, the capacity to learn lessons is more valuable than any individual lesson learned. That capacity is what companies can gain by studying OPFOR.

The AAR in Practice and Its Payoff

	The AAR in practice	The payoff
1. Emergency response	• Survey past emergencies to identify types of events and learning challenges. • Ask team members to take notes during the response process to facilitate the upcoming AAR. • Conduct AARs during the response process (if possible) or immediately afterward to begin building procedures and long-term solutions. • Periodically review past AARs to identify potential systems improvements.	• Avoid similar emergencies in the future. • Improve the speed and quality of your responses and damage control. • Improve the long-term effectiveness of your solutions.
2. Product development	• Start each phase of product development with a before-action review (BAR). • Conduct AARs to identify insights to feed from one phase of product development into the next—and then into the next project. • Periodically conduct AARs on the product-planning process to identify potential improvements.	• Improve quality, reduce cost, and shorten time to market. • Anticipate customers' changing expectations.

3. Entering a new business or market	• Launch business planning with a BAR to reflect on past lessons. • Conduct AARs throghout the launch process to test lessons and create innovative solutions. • Conduct a wrap-up AAR to improve performance on the next venture.	• Apply lessons from past successes and failures to improve results on new ventures.
4. Sales	• Build AARs into the sales process, focusing as much on learning from wins as from losses. • Conduct AARs on customer defections to competitors' products.	• Improve the win/loss ratio. • Refine the value proposition for a new product.
5. Mergers and acquisitions	• Build AARs into strategy, negotiation, due diligence, and execution phases to continually reveal, test, and modify assumptions about the deal. • Wrap up each M&A activity by comparing it with previous efforts to identify problems and good ideas.	• Ensure that transactions deliver promised value to stakeholders.

Learning to Be OPFOR

THE 11TH ARMORED CAVALRY REGIMENT (ACR),
which has played the Opposing Force (OPFOR) for
more than a decade, is a brigade of regular U.S. Army
soldiers. In the current environment, every Army unit that
is deployable has been activated—including the 11th
ACR, which is now overseas.

It will return. In the meantime, a National Guard unit
that fought side by side with the 11th ACR for ten years
has assumed the OPFOR mantle. This new OPFOR faces
even greater challenges than the regular brigade did. It
is smaller. It comprises not professional soldiers but week-
end warriors from such companies as UPS and Nextel.
And it recently gave up its home-court advantage and
traveled to BLUFOR's home base when that unit-in-
training's deployment date was moved up.

Nonetheless, the Army is satisfied that this new
OPFOR—now one year into its role—is successfully
preparing combat units for deployment to the Middle
East. It has managed that, in large part, by leveraging
the after-action review (AAR) regimen it learned from the
11th ACR. It is difficult to imagine a more dramatic
change than the wholesale replacement of one team by
another. That the new OPFOR has met this challenge is
powerful evidence of the AAR's efficacy to help an organization learn and adapt quickly.

Five Ways to Put AARs to Work at Work

THE U.S. ARMY'S STANDING ENEMY BRIGADE
(referred to as OPFOR) applies the after-action review

(AAR) process to everything it does, but that's not realistic for most companies. Business leaders must act selectively, with an eye toward resources and potential payoffs. Don't even think about creating an AAR regimen without determining who is likely to learn from it and how they will benefit. Build slowly, beginning with activities where the payoff is greatest and where leaders have committed to working through several AAR cycles. Focus on areas critical to a team's mission so members have good reason to participate. And customize the process to fit each project and project phase. For example, during periods of intense activity, brief daily AAR meetings can help teams coordinate and improve the next day's activities. At other times, meetings might occur monthly or quarterly and be used to identify exceptions in volumes of operational data and to understand the causes. The level of activity should always match the potential value of lessons learned. The exhibit, "The AAR in Practice and Its Payoff," shows some ways you can use AARs, based on examples from companies that have used them effectively.

Doctrine and Tactics

THE LESSONS PRODUCED and validated by the U.S. Army's Opposing Force (OPFOR) and the units it trains at the National Training Center (NTC) in Fort Irwin, California, contribute to the Army's two classes of organizational knowledge. One class, known as Tactics, Techniques, and Procedures (TTP), focuses on how to perform specific tasks under specific conditions. It is the responsibility of each unit leader to build her own library of TTP by learning from other leaders as well as by capturing good ideas from her subordinates. Two unit leaders in the same brigade may need to employ different TTP to address different conditions.

Sufficiently weighty, widely applicable, and rigorously tested TTP may ultimately inform the Army's other class of organizational knowledge: doctrine. Doctrine—which rarely changes and is shared by the entire Army—establishes performance standards for the kinds of actions and conditions military units commonly face. For example, many of the steps in the doctrine for a brigade-level attack (such as planning for mobility, survivability, and air defense) began life as lessons from the NTC and other Army training centers.

The difference between doctrine and TTP is a useful one for businesses, some of which draw few distinctions among the types of knowledge employees generate and about how widely diverse lessons should be applied and disseminated.

Originally published in July–August 2005
Reprint R0507G

Collaboration Rules

PHILIP EVANS AND BOB WOLF

Executive Summary

CORPORATE LEADERS SEEKING TO BOOST GROWTH, learning, and innovation may find the answer in a surprising place: the Linux open-source software community. Linux is developed by an essentially volunteer, self-organizing community of thousands of programmers. Most leaders would sell their grandmothers for workforces that collaborate as efficiently, frictionlessly, and creatively as the self-styled Linux hackers.

But Linux is software, and software is hardly a model for mainstream business. The authors have, nonetheless, found surprising parallels between the anarchistic, caffeinated, hirsute world of Linux hackers and the disciplined, tea-sipping, clean-cut world of Toyota engineering.

Specifically, Toyota and Linux operate by rules that blend the self-organizing advantages of markets with the low transaction costs of hierarchies. In place of markets' cash and contracts and hierarchies' authority are rules about how individuals and groups work together (with rigorous discipline); how they communicate (widely and with granularity); and how leaders guide them toward a common goal (through example).

Those rules, augmented by simple communication technologies and a lack of legal barriers to sharing information, create rich common knowledge, the ability to organize teams modularly, extraordinary motivation, and high levels of trust, which radically lowers transaction costs. Low transaction costs, in turn, make it profitable for organizations to perform more and smaller transactions—and so increase the pace and flexibility typical of high-performance organizations.

Once the system achieves critical mass, it feeds on itself. The larger the system, the more broadly shared the knowledge, language, and work style. The greater individuals' reputational capital, the louder the applause and the stronger the motivation. The success of Linux is evidence of the power of that virtuous circle. Toyota's success is evidence that it is also powerful in conventional companies.

CORPORATE LEADERS SEEKING GROWTH, learning, and innovation may find the answer in a surprising place: the open-source software community. Unknowingly, perhaps, the folks who brought you Linux are virtuoso practitioners of new work principles that produce energized teams and lower costs. Nor are they alone.

By any measure, Linux is a powerfully competitive product. It is estimated that more servers run on Linux than on any other operating system. It has over-whelmed UNIX as a commercial offering. And its advantages extend beyond cost and quality to the speed with which it is enhanced and improved. While partisans debate its technical limitations and treatment of intellectual property, they agree that the product's success is inseparable from its distinctive mode of production. Specifically, Linux is the creation of an essentially voluntary, self-organizing community of thousands of programmers and companies. Most leaders would sell their grandmothers for workforces that collaborate as efficiently, frictionlessly, and creatively as the self-styled Linux "hackers."

But Linux is software, and software is kind of weird. Toyota, however, is a company like any other—any other consistently ranked among the world's top-performing organizations, that is. The automaker has long been a leader in quality and lean production, and the success of the hybrid Prius has established its reputation as an innovator. We have found that Toyota's managerial methods resemble, in a number of their fundamentals, the workings of the Linux community; the Toyota Production System (TPS) owes some of its vaunted responsiveness to open-source traits. In fact, Toyota itself is evolving into a hybrid between a conventional hierarchy and a Linux-like self-organizing network.

(Throughout this article, we use the term "Linux" as shorthand for the free/open-source software community that developed and continues to refine the operating system and other open-source programs. We use "Toyota" as shorthand for the Toyota Production System, which comprises Toyota and its direct—"tier one" in automotive parlance—suppliers in Japan and the United States.)

Toyota is remarkably similar to Linux in the way it blends key characteristics of both markets and hierarchies. Like markets, the Toyota and Linux communities can be self-organizing, but unlike markets, they don't use cash or contracts at critical junctures. Like hierarchies, Toyota and Linux enjoy low transaction costs, but unlike hierarchies, their members may belong to many different organizations (or to none at all) and are not corseted by specific, predefined roles and responsibilities. And like hierarchies, members share a common purpose, but that purpose emanates from self-motivation rather than from the external incentives or sanctions that hierarchies generally impose. In these respects, Toyota and Linux represent the best of both worlds. An analysis of their common characteristics suggests how high-performance organizations remain productive and inventive even under grueling conditions. We believe those lessons can significantly improve the way work in most organizations gets done.

Tuesday, December 2, 2003

Near midnight, Andrea Barisani, system administrator in the physics department of the University of Trieste, discovered that an attacker had struck his institution's Gentoo Linux server. He traced the breach to a vulnerable spot in the Linux kernel and another in rsync, a file transfer mechanism that automatically replicates data among computers. This was a serious attack: Any penetration of rsync could compromise files in thousands of servers worldwide.

Barisani woke some colleagues, who put him in touch with Mike Warfield, a senior researcher at Inter-

net Security Systems in Atlanta, and with Andrew
"Tridge" Tridgell, a well-known Linux programmer in
Australia on whose doctoral thesis rsync was based.
They directed Barisani's message (made anonymous for
security reasons) to another Australian, Martin Pool,
who worked for Hewlett-Packard in Canberra and had
been a leader in rsync's development. Although Pool
was no longer responsible for rsync (nobody was), he
immediately hit the phones and e-mail, first quizzing
Warfield and Dave Dykstra (another early contributor
to rsync's development, who was based in California)
about vulnerabilities and then helping Barisani trace
the failure line by line.

By morning Trieste time, Pool and Barisani had found
the precise location of the breach. Pool contacted the
current rsync development group, while Barisani connected with the loose affiliation of amateurs and professionals that package Gentoo Linux, and he posted an
early warning advisory to the Gentoo site. Pool and Paul
"Rusty" Russell (a fellow Canberran who works for IBM)
then labored through the Australian night to write a
patch, and within five hours Gentoo user-developers
started testing the first version. Meanwhile, Tridge
crafted a description of the vulnerability and its fix, being
sure (at Pool's urging) to credit Barisani and Warfield for
their behind-the-scenes efforts. On Thursday afternoon
Canberra time, the announcement and the patch were
posted to the rsync Web site and thus distributed to
Linux users worldwide.

A few days after the emergency, having caught up on
his sleep, Barisani volunteered to collaborate with
Warfield in setting up a system of deliberately vulnerable
servers to lure the system cracker into revealing himself.

No one authorized or directed this effort. No one—amateur or professional—was paid for participating or would have been sanctioned for not doing so. No one's job hinged on stopping the attack. No one clammed up for fear of legal liability. Indeed, the larger user community was kept informed of all developments. Yet despite the need for the highest security, a group of some 20 people, scarcely any of whom had ever met, employed by a dozen different companies, living in as many time zones and straying far from their job descriptions, accomplished in about 29 hours what might have taken colleagues in adjacent cubicles weeks or months.

It's tempting to dismiss this as an example of hacker weirdness—admirable, yes, but nothing to do with real business. Consider, however, another story.

Saturday, February 1, 1997

At 4:18 AM, a fire broke out in the Kariya Number 1 plant of Aisin Seiki, a major Japanese automotive parts supplier. Within minutes, the building and virtually all the specialized machinery inside were destroyed. Kariya Number 1 produces 99 percent of the brake fluid–proportioning valves, or P-valves, for Toyota's Japanese operations—parts required by every vehicle Toyota builds. And Toyota, true to its just-in-time principles, had less than a day's inventory. The Japanese Toyota Production System faced the possibility of a total shutdown lasting months.

Within hours, Aisin engineers met with their counterparts at Toyota and Toyota's other tier one suppliers. The group agreed to improvise as much production as possible. As news spread through the supplier network, some tier twos volunteered to play leadership roles. Aisin sent blueprints for the valves to any supplier that requested them and distributed whatever undamaged tools, raw materials, and work in process could be salvaged. Aisin and Toyota engineers helped jury-rig production lines in 62 locations—unused machine shops, Toyota's own prototyping shop, even a sewing machine facility owned by Brother. Denso, Toyota's largest supplier, volunteered to manage the messy logistics of shipping valves to Aisin for inspection and then on to Toyota's stalled assembly lines.

Everyone was surprised when a small tier two supplier of welding electrodes, Kyoritsu Sangyo, was first to deliver production-quality valves to Toyota—1,000 of them, just 85 hours after the fire. Others followed rapidly, and Toyota started reopening assembly lines on Wednesday. Roughly two weeks after the halt, the entire supply chain was back to full production. Six months later, Aisin distributed an emergency response guide containing lessons drawn from the experience and recommending procedures for responding to such situations in the future.

No one individual or organization planned this effort: rather, people and companies stepped in where they could. Competitors collaborated. No one at the time was paid for contributing. Months later, Aisin compensated the other companies for the direct costs of the valves they had delivered. Toyota gave each tier one supplier an honorarium based on current sales to the automaker, encouraging—but not requiring—them to do likewise for their own tier twos.

Few communities appear more different than the anarchistic, caffeinated, hirsute world of hackers and the disciplined, tea-sipping, clean-cut world of Japanese auto engineering. But the parallels between these stories are striking. In both of them, individuals found one another and stepped into roles without a plan or an established command-and-control structure. An extended human network organized itself in hours and "swarmed" against a threat. People, teams, and companies worked together without legal contracts or negotiated payment. And despite the lack of any authoritarian stick or financial carrot, those people worked *like hell* to solve the problem.

Now, obviously, these were emergency responses. But a look at the day-to-day operations of the Linux community and the Toyota Production System reveals that those responses were merely intensifications of the way people were already working.

Obsession, Interaction, and a Light Touch

The rules of markets are about cash and contracts. The rules of hierarchies are about authority and accountability. But at the core of the Linux and Toyota communities are rules about three entirely different things: how individuals and small groups work together; how, and how widely, they communicate; and how leaders guide them toward a common goal.

A COMMON WORK DISCIPLINE

The Linux and Toyota communities are both composed of engineers, so members have the same skills as their colleagues and speak the same language. But these groups are far more disciplined and rigorous in their approach to work than are other engineering communities. Both emphasize granularity: They pay attention to small details, eliminate problems at the source, and trim anything resembling excess, whether it be work, code, or material. Linux members, for example, share an obsession with writing minimal code, compiling each day's output before proceeding to the next and extirpating programming flaws as they go along. For their part, TPS engineers are relentless in applying short cycles of trial and error, focusing on just one thing at a time, and getting inside and observing actual processes. Both groups carry those principles to apparent extremes. Linux programmers whittle away at code in pursuit not of computational efficiency but of elegance. Toyota engineers reject stampings for the Lexus hood—while flawless and entirely within spec—because the sheen, to their eyes, lacks luster.

WIDESPREAD, GRANULAR COMMUNICATION

In both the Linux and Toyota communities, information about problems and solutions is shared widely, frequently, and in small increments. Most Linux hacker communication is not between individuals but by postings to open, searchable Listservs. Anyone can review the version history of the code and the Listserv debates—not executive summaries or abstracts but the raw activity itself. And every code contribution is stress tested by scores of people. As a famous open-source mixed metaphor puts it: "With a thousand eyes, all bugs are shallow." The median upload to the Linux kernel is a mere dozen lines of code. The working alpha version is recompiled every 24 hours, so hackers reconcile their efforts almost continuously. If someone worked in isolation for six months on even the most brilliant contribution, it would probably be rejected for lack of compatibility with the others' efforts.

The Toyota philosophy of continuous improvement likewise comprises a thousand small collaborations. Toyota engineers are famously drilled to "ask why five times" to follow a chain of causes and effects back to a problem's root. This is not a vapid cliché about thinking deeply. Quite the contrary, in fact. The precept's merit is precisely in its superficiality. Saying that B causes A is simplistic-all the complexities of multiple interactions boiled down to a single cause and effect. But the chain of thought required to discover that C causes B, and D causes C, quickly takes you into a new domain, probably someone else's. So rather than concoct complex solutions within their own domains, engineers must seek simple ones beyond them. "Doing your why-whys," as the practice is known, is not about depth at all—it's about breadth.

And as with Linux, Toyota's communication protocols enforce this discipline. Each meeting addresses just one topic and drives toward a specific outcome, even if that means the same people meet more than once in a day. Lessons are written in a standard format on a single sheet of A3 paper. And everyone learns how to craft these reports, down to the fold in the document that shows the main points and conceals the details.

LEADERS AS CONNECTORS

At every level, Linux and TPS leaders play three critical roles. They instruct community members—often by example—in the disciplines we've just described. They articulate clear and simple goals for each project based on their strategic vision. And they connect people, by merit of being very well connected themselves. The top Linux programmers process upwards of 300 or 400 e-mails daily. Fujio Cho, the president of Toyota, manages by similarly numerous daily interactions that transcend the normal chain of command.

Neither community treats leading as a discipline distinct from doing. Rather, the credibility and, therefore, authority of leaders derives from their proficiency as practitioners. The content of leaders' staccato communications is less *about* work than it *is* work. (When Linux creator Linus Torvalds dashes off his scores of daily e-mails, he writes almost as much in the C programming language as he does in English.)

Occasionally, leaders do have to perform traditional leadership acts, such as arbitrating conflicts. That, however, is the exception and is viewed as a bit of a system failure. The default assumption is that, as far as possible, managers don't manage in a traditional sense: The human network manages itself. In Linux, development priorities are decided not by a CEO but by thousands of hackers voting with their feet by choosing what to work on. That kind of radical self-management does not happen at Toyota, except in emergencies. But even in daily operations, a single production worker who sees a quality problem can stop the line, and project teams have wide latitude to tap resources, make purchase decisions, and pursue priorities they set for themselves.

Taken together, these three principles seed a continuously adapting system. Over and over, ideas are formulated in tight, testable packets; they are communicated with minimal attenuation through established, direct, person-to-person connections; and where links are absent, widely connected leader-practitioners create them as needed. This is discipline, but not the discipline of conformity produced by controls and incentives. Rather, it resembles the discipline of science. Like scientific communities, these systems rely on common procedures, common rules for communication and testing, and common goals clearly understood. Individual behavior is rigorously cautious, but collective achievement is marked by continuous, radical innovation.

What They Know and How They Know It

At the heart of Linux and the Toyota Production System, then, is a set of work, communication, and leadership practices that contributes to a new form of collaboration. This collaboration also relies on two infrastructure components: a shared pool of knowledge and universally available tools for moving knowledge around.

COMMON INTELLECTUAL PROPERTY

The General Public License under which Linux is published requires that all distributors make their source code freely available so that others can freely emend it. This viral principle prevents code from being stowed away in proprietary products. That transparency, in turn, breaks down the distinction between producer and user. A sophisticated "customer" like Andrea Barisani is really a user-developer, who fixes flaws and adds features for his own benefit, then shares those improvements with everyone else. Such a role is impossible when proprietary code is licensed from a commercial vendor. Similarly, Toyota's supply chain is predicated on the principle that while product knowledge (such as a blueprint) is someone's intellectual property, process knowledge is shared. That breaks down some distinctions among companies. Toyota's suppliers regularly share extensive process improvement lessons both vertically and laterally, even with their competitors. In Japan, suppliers are generally exclusive to a single OEM, so the collective benefit of that shared information stays within the Toyota supply chain. But even in the United States, where Toyota is just one of several customers for most of its tier ones, the carmaker does the same thing through its Bluegrass Automotive Manufacturers Association, which disseminates best practices to all members.

SIMPLE, PERVASIVE TECHNOLOGY

Although information is the lifeblood of the Linux and TPS communities, their circulation systems are surprisingly rudimentary. Linux developers produce state-of-the-art software using communication technology no more sophisticated than e-mail and Listservs—but those mundane tools are used by everyone. Indeed, so great is the value placed on universality that plain-text, rather than formatted, e-mails are the norm, ensuring that messages will appear exactly the same to all recipients. Toyota, whose products are state-of-the-art as well, also prefers simple and pervasive internal technology. An empty kanban bin signals the need for parts replenishment; a length of duct tape on the assembly-line floor allots the completion times of tasks on a moving vehicle. Quality control problems on the assembly line are announced via pagers and TV monitors. And everyone gets the alert. Even Ray Tanguay, head of Toyota Canada, is paged whenever a flaw is found in the latest Lexus consignment on the dock in Long Beach, California, or in a service bay anywhere in North America.

The Power of Trust and Applause

Such extremely rich, flexible collaborations have positive psychological consequences for participants and powerful competitive ones for their organizations. Those consequences are rich common knowledge, the ability to organize teams modularly, extraordinary motivation, and high levels of trust.

RICH SEMANTIC KNOWLEDGE

A rigorous work discipline, common intellectual property, and constant sharing combine to distribute knowledge widely and relatively evenly across human networks. That knowledge includes not just the formal, syntactic information found in databases but also the semantically rich, ambiguous knowledge about content and process that is the currency of creative collaboration. What do we mean by the sheen of a body stamping having insufficient luster? What, precisely, must we discuss with the steel company to correct such an ill-defined problem? This kind of no-easy-answer question is continually discussed and resolved in a thousand small-team collaborations. The resulting nuanced thinking and richer common vocabulary on such matters are fed back into the knowledge pool, where they are available for further refinement by the whole community.

MODULAR TEAMING

Modularity is a design principle by which a complex process or product is divided into simple parts connected by standard rules. In modular arrangements of teams, each team focuses on small, simple tasks that together make up a larger whole. Modularity allows an organization to run multiple, parallel experiments, making many small bets instead of a few large ones. The Toyota suppliers organized themselves this way to make P-valves, operating partly by direction but chiefly by volunteering to do what each knew best. The Gentoo group, Tridge's security experts, and Pool's circle of rsync alumni were preexisting and overlapping modules that mixed and matched roles as the emergency required.

When we mapped the patterns of day-to-day collaboration across the entire Linux kernel development effort, we found that such modular arrangements are pervasive and, to a degree, nest within one another. This creates a kind of dynamic organization chart—a chart that nobody wrote but one that enables the community to expand and adapt without collapsing into chaos.

INTRINSIC MOTIVATION

The Linux and TPS communities dissociate money from key transactions. Yet despite weak financial incentives, they command a level of motivation higher than that found in conventional environments. Monetary carrots and accountability sticks, psychologists have consistently found, motivate people to perform narrow, specified tasks but generally discourage people from going beyond them. Admiration and applause are far more effective stimulants of above-and-beyond behavior. "The personal reputation of the developer is attached to every release," Linus Torvalds explained to technology columnist Robert Cringely in 1998. "If you are making something to give away to the world, something that represents to millions of users your philosophy of computing, you will always make it the very best product you can."

Psychologists also emphasize the motivational importance of autonomy. Linux programmers decide for themselves how and where to contribute, and they enjoy the satisfaction of producing something whose quality is defined not by a marketing department nor by accountants but by their own exacting standards. Coauthor Bob Wolf and MIT's Karim Lakhani surveyed more than 800 user-developers, and over half said that their open-source work is the most valuable and creative endeavor in their professional lives.

The Toyota Production System doesn't offer such extreme autonomy, of course, and employees don't work for free. But compared with their counterparts in the rest of the auto industry, TPS workers enjoy fewer controls, greater encouragement of individual initiative, fewer metrics attached to individual performance, and louder peer applause. Professional and corporate pride, not Toyota's honorarium, was the payoff for the team at Kyoritsu Sangyo when it delivered the first batch of P-valves. That same pride is felt by a junior assembly-line worker when he is trusted by his peers to experiment with process improvements and to stop the line if something goes wrong.

HIGH LEVELS OF TRUST

When information flows freely, reputation, more than reciprocity, becomes the basis for trust. Operating under constant scrutiny—which is challenging but not hostile—workers know their reputations are at risk, and that serves as a guarantor of good behavior, the equivalent of contracts in a market or audits in a hierarchy. Hence the obsession in the Linux community with acknowledging code contributions and including personal e-mail addresses in the comment fields of Listservs. Hence the generous public credit bestowed on Barisani and Warfield. Hence the collective celebration of Kyoritsu Sangyo's heroic efforts.

With their reputations at stake, people are less likely to act opportunistically. With the same information available to everyone, there is less chance that one party will exploit another's ignorance. And with a common vocabulary and way of working, fewer misunderstandings occur. Those factors drive up trust, the fundamental social capital of these communities.

Trust would matter less if there were no cost to exiting these networks or if transactions were of radically different sizes (since that would tempt people or companies to break the rules when a big opportunity arose). But in both the Linux and Toyota communities, entry to the inner circle is a hard-earned privilege, and both operate on many small exchanges.

And, of course, where trust is the currency, reputation is a source of power. In a sparse network, such as most markets and hierarchies, power derives from controlling or brokering the flow of information and often, therefore, from restricting it. In a dense network, however, information simply flows around the would-be choke point. Under those circumstances, there is more power in being an information source than an information sink. Consequently, individuals are motivated to maximize both the visibility of their work and their connections to those who are themselves broadly connected. That, in turn, feeds the information density of the network.

Cheap Transactions and Plenty of Them

So far we have been discussing the content of work. But the TPS and Linux models change the economics of work as well, by driving down transaction costs. Low transaction costs make it profitable for organizations to perform more and smaller transactions—both internal and external—and so increase the pace and flexibility typical of high-performance organizations.

The classical sources of transaction costs are mutual vulnerability in the face of uncertainty, conflicting interests, and unequal access to information. We spend cash on negotiation, supervision, and restitution to reduce those imperfections. Both markets and hierarchies incur transaction costs (though hierarchies exist to economize on them, as Ronald Coase and Oliver Williamson have argued). Using a methodology developed by J.J. Wallis and Douglass North, we estimate that in the year 2000, cash transaction costs alone accounted for over half the nongovernmental U.S. GDP! We spend more money negotiating and enforcing transactions than we do fulfilling them.

In the Linux and Toyota communities, agreements are enforced not by the sanction of a legal contract, nor by the authority of a boss, but by mutual trust—lowering transaction costs dramatically. This is not new: Teams of people everywhere in the conventional workplace operate on the basis of trust.

What is new is how widely trust can extend, even to people who don't know each other—or even among those who have competing interests. Aisin trusted its rival suppliers with the P-valve blueprints. The rsync hackers swapped sensitive information with people they had never met. Toyota's component suppliers share process knowledge daily, trusting that Toyota will not use it to beat down prices. Linux hackers trust one another to make uncoordinated and simultaneous emendations in the code base.

Moreover, holding property in common—as certain kinds of intellectual property are held within these communities—lowers the monetary stakes among the joint owners. Transaction costs fall because there is simply less to negotiate over. In the Linux community, transaction costs approach zero. Hewlett-Packard paid Martin Pool to be a Linux engineer, but it does not follow that HP needed to be paid on the margin for Pool's nocturnal labors on rsync. In the Toyota community, transaction costs, while not zero, have been radically reduced. When the Aisin Seiki plant was destroyed, Toyota and its suppliers didn't sue one another or cobble together emergency supply contracts. They simply got on with the job, trusting that fair restitution would eventually be made. Jeffrey Dyer, a professor of strategy at Brigham Young University, estimates that transaction costs between Toyota and its tier one suppliers are just one-eighth those at General Motors, a disparity he attributes to different levels of trust.

A Model for Many

Bring together all these elements and you have a virtuous circle. A dense, self-organizing network creates the conditions for large-scale trust. Large-scale trust drives down transaction costs. Low transaction costs, in turn, enable lots of small transactions, which create a cumulatively deepening, self-organized network.

Once the system achieves critical mass, it feeds on itself. The larger the system, the more broadly shared the knowledge, language, and work style. The greater individuals' reputational capital, the louder the applause and the stronger the motivation. The success of Linux is evidence of the power of that virtuous circle. Toyota's success is evidence that it is also powerful in conventional, profit-maximizing companies.

The Linux community and Toyota Production System are strikingly different. The fact that they achieve so much in such similar ways points to some principles others can follow.

- The discipline of science is surprisingly adaptable to the organization of corporate—and even intercorporate—work.

- Under some circumstances, trust is a viable substitute for market contracts and hierarchical authority, not just in small teams but also in very large communities.

- Across supply chains, organizations that are able to substitute trust for contracts gain more from the collaboration than they lose in bargaining power.

- Low transaction costs buy more innovation than do high monetary incentives.

These principles serve businesses' need for growth and innovation in ways that traditional organizational models do not. And perhaps the effectiveness of these collaborations suggests the ultimate emergence of something altogether new. Not markets. Not hierarchies. But a powerful combination of both—and a signature of the networked society.

Building Vibrant Human Networks

COMPANIES LAYING THE GROUNDWORK for high-performance collaboration should follow these principles:

- **Deploy pervasive collaborative technology.** Keep it simple and open: "small pieces loosely joined," in *Cluetrain Manifesto* coauthor David Weinberger's felicitous phrase. Tools should work together through common standards and be as compatible as possible with those of the rest of the world. Think options not integration, adaptability not static efficiency.

- **Keep work visible.** Unless there is a really good reason not to, let everybody see everybody's real work. Let people learn to filter and sort for themselves. Don't abstract, summarize, or channel. Fodder is good. Put it within everyone's reach.

- **Build communities of trust.** When people trust one another, they are more likely to collaborate freely and productively. When people trust their organizations, they are more likely to give of themselves now in anticipation of future reward. And when organizations trust each other, they are more likely to share intellectual property without choking on legalisms.

- **Think modularly.** Reengineering was about thinking linearly: managing the end-to-end process instead of discrete functions. That approach fosters focused efficiency but inhibits variety and adaptability. Modularity is the reverse: sacrificing static efficiency for the recombinant value of options. Think modular teams as well as processes. The finer, the better.

- **Encourage teaming.** Celebrate the sacrifices that teams make for the broader enterprise, including customers and suppliers. Dismantle individualized performance metrics and rewards that pit people against one another. Cheap transactions among the many fuel more innovation than expensive incentives aimed at the few. Reward the group, and the group will reward you.

Exploiting the Neglected 80%

THE PARETO PRINCIPLE famously dictates that companies derive 80% of their value from just 20% of their products, customers, or ideas. Because of high transaction costs, the long tail of that curve—that 80% of uncertain value generators—cannot be explored. So in the name of company focus, the tail gets lopped off, segmented away, or reengineered out of existence. Potentially profitable innovations die with it.

Organizations that reduce transaction costs can embrace the rejected 80%. They can respond to weak market signals, tap small segments, and experiment with unlikely combinations of technologies. They can place a hundred small bets instead of a few big ones.

For example, Detroit considered hybrid vehicles to be an uninteresting intermediate product: U.S. auto executives preferred so-far-unfulfilled research on fuel cell technology. Meanwhile, Toyota was building the Prius. The hybrid is now in its second generation, and Toyota expects to sell 300,000 worldwide this year. Toyota's low transaction costs and penchant for small-scale collaborations helped it keep open 80 discrete options for the hybrid engine until just six months before delivering a final design. Conventional automakers would have needed to freeze those design variables at least two years earlier.

It is in the interstices of the human network—rather than in the minds of a few wunderkinder—that most real innovations are born. And so it is transaction costs that constrain innovation by constraining opportunities to share different and conflicting ideas, skills, and prejudices.

"Detroit people are far more talented than people at Toyota," remarks Toyota president Fujio Cho, with excessive modesty. "But we take averagely talented people and make them work as spectacular teams." The network, in other words, is the innovator.

Giving Credit Where Credit Is Due

THE LINUX COMMUNITY uses a particular format— a "credit file"—to acknowledge the contributions of its members. If we, for instance, were to acknowledge in the Linux format the contributions of individuals who helped shape our thinking for this article, here's how it would look:

n: Mark Blaxill

e: blaxill.mark@bcg.com

d: Exploration of economics of open source

s: Boston Consulting Group

n: Paul Carlile

e: carlile@bu.edu

d: Discussion of Linux/Toyota parallels

s: Boston University

n: Karim Lakhani

e: lakhani@mit.edu

d: Discussion of Linux/Toyota parallels

d: Survey of free/open source hackers

s: MIT

Originally published in July–August 2005
Reprint R0507H

Manage Your Human Sigma

JOHN H. FLEMING, CURT COFFMAN,
AND JAMES K. HARTER

Executive Summary

IF SALES AND SERVICE ORGANIZATIONS are to
improve, they must learn to measure and manage the
quality of the employee-customer encounter. Quality
improvement methodologies such as Six Sigma are
extremely useful in manufacturing contexts, but they're
less useful when it comes to human interactions. To
address this problem, the authors have developed a
quality improvement approach they refer to as Human
Sigma. It weaves together a consistent method for
assessing the employee-customer encounter and a disciplined process for managing and improving it.

There are several core principles for measuring and
managing the employee-customer encounter: It's important not to think like an economist or an engineer when
assessing interactions because emotions inform both
sides' judgments and behavior. The employee-customer

encounter must be measured and managed locally, because there are enormous variations in quality at the work-group and individual levels. And to improve the quality of the employee-customer interaction, organizations must conduct both short-term, transactional interventions and long-term, transformational ones.

Employee engagement and customer engagement are intimately connected—and, taken together, they have an outsized effect on financial performance. They therefore need to be managed holistically. That is, the responsibility for measuring and monitoring the health of employee-customer relationships must reside within a single organizational structure, with an executive champion who has the authority to initiate and manage change. Nevertheless, the local manager remains the single most important factor in local group performance. A local manager whose work group shows suboptimal performance should be encouraged to conduct interventions, such as targeted training, performance reviews, action learning, and individual coaching.

"QUALITY" IS EASY TO MEASURE and manage in some contexts, and extremely difficult in others. Businesspeople have a pretty good idea how to judge the manufacturing process that yields a snazzy new handheld device, for example. But what about the retail employee's attempts to sell the gadget? Or the call center employee's efforts to help the customer navigate its eccentricities? Businesses aren't especially good at measuring and managing the quality of those processes—or indeed of most work done by nonmanufacturing businesses and units."

Yet it's essential that organizations learn to measure and manage quality in *all* kinds of business settings. In manufacturing, value is created on the factory floor. In sales and service organizations, and in many professional service firms, value is created when an employee interacts with a customer. Indeed, the employee-customer encounter *is* the factory floor of sales and services. If these organizations are going to achieve meaningful operational and financial improvements, the employee-customer encounter must be managed with great care.

Quality improvement methodologies such as Six Sigma are extremely useful in manufacturing contexts, where ingredients with predictable properties are repeatedly combined in the same ways, but they're less useful when it comes to the employee-customer encounter, with its volatile human dimensions. To address this problem of fit, we've developed a quality improvement approach that we call Human Sigma. Like Six Sigma, Human Sigma focuses on reducing variability and improving performance. But while Six Sigma applies to processes, systems, and output quality, our approach looks at the quality of the employee-customer encounter, weaving together a consistent method for assessing it and a disciplined process for managing and improving it.

As we developed our thinking about Human Sigma, we arrived at several core principles for measuring and managing interactions between customers and employees:

- It's important not to think like an economist or an engineer when you're assessing the employee-customer interaction. Emotions, it turns out, inform both sides' judgments and behavior even more powerfully than rationality does.

- The employee-customer encounter must be measured and managed locally, because there are enormous variations in quality at the work-group and individual levels.

- It's possible to arrive at a single measure of effectiveness for the employee-customer encounter; this measure has a high correlation with financial performance.

- To improve the quality of the employee-customer interaction, organizations must conduct both short-term, transactional interventions (such as coaching) and long-term, transformational ones (such as changing the processes for hiring and promotion). In addition, the company's organizational structure often must be adjusted so that the employee-customer encounter can be managed holistically.

Human Sigma grew out of a multiyear, research-based initiative designed to map the terrain of the employee-customer encounter. We identified ways to measure the effectiveness of the encounter, explored how those metrics could best be used, and assessed the benefits that could result from their application. This work was based on direct experience with hundreds of companies and millions of customers and employees. We then tested and cross-validated our findings in 1,979 business units—involved in financial services, professional services, retail, and sales—within ten companies. The results thus far have been extraordinary. The ten companies, all of which have applied the best-practice principles for managing the employee-customer encounter, together outperformed their five largest peers during 2003 by 26 percent in gross margins and by 85 percent in sales growth. We can't guarantee readers comparable results, but we believe that closely monitoring the health of a firm's employee-customer relationships will result in dramatic performance improvements.

Emotions Frame the Encounter

Six Sigma processes are data driven, rational, and analytic. They focus on conformance to requirements, which are generally specified in functional terms. Does the product have any defects? Are its parameters within specified manufacturing tolerances? Is it delivered on time? Widespread use of Six Sigma and TQM methodologies has resulted in vastly improved product quality over the past two decades.

Inspired by these improvements, businesses have tried to apply Six Sigma principles in sales and service settings. In early attempts, researchers and managers alike assumed that the customers in those settings would be as focused on conformance to requirements as the engineers on the factory floor were. Had this been the case—had customers been rational creatures who judged their interactions with company representatives using rigorous, analytical standards—then simple flawlessness on the company's part would have resulted in satisfied, profitable, lifelong customers.

But nothing human is ever that simple. People may think that their behavior is purely rational, but it rarely is. Twenty years of research in two very different fields— neuroscience and behavioral economics—has established quite clearly that people base their decisions on a complicated mixture of emotion and reason. Indeed, recent work suggests that emotions may play a larger role than analysis.

CUSTOMER ENGAGEMENT

That work in neuroscience and behavioral economics is
borne out by research into customer satisfaction and
engagement. Results from a large and growing number of
case studies suggest that "extremely satisfied" customers
(people who provide the highest rating of overall satisfaction with a company's products and services) fall into
two distinct groups: those who have a strong emotional
connection to the company and those who do not. When
we examine indicators of customer behavior (such as
attrition, frequency of use, total revenue, and total
spending), a clear and striking pattern emerges. Emotionally satisfied customers contribute far more to the
bottom line than rationally satisfied customers do, even
though they are equally "satisfied." In fact, the behavior
of rationally satisfied customers looks no different from
that of *dissatisfied* customers. The pattern shown in the
exhibit "Emotional Satisfaction Matters Most" has
emerged in every study we have examined.

Imagine that you could peek inside the heads of your
customers as they thought about your company. Would
people with a strong emotional connection to the firm
show different brain activity than other customers? As
it turns out, the answer is yes. We studied three groups
of customers of a luxury retailer in Japan. One group
was strongly attached emotionally (according to our
measure of emotional attachment), one was moderately
attached, and the third had little or no attachment.
While inside a functional magnetic resonance imaging
(fMRI) machine, the customers responded to simple
agree-or-disagree statements about the retailer, about
their bank, and about various aspects of daily life. The

Emotional Satisfaction Matters Most

At a large U.S. retail bank, the attrition rate of dissatisfied customers was scarely different from that of "rationally satisfied" customers, those who describe themselves as extremely satisfied but scored low on an emotional-attachment metric that measures four dimensions—confidence, integrity, pride, and passion. By contrast, the attrition rate of people who were "emotionally satisfied" by the bank was, on average, 37% lower. Similarly, dissatisfied customers of an international credit card provider were virtually indistinguishable from rationally satisfied cardholders in their purchase behavior, while customers who were emotionally satisfied by factors such as service, features, and brand image spent more, on average, than people in the other groups. (The emotionally satisfied group also increased its spending by 67% over 12 months, compared with 8% for the rationally satisfied group; there was a small decrease within the dissatisfied group.)

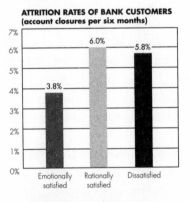

ATTRITION RATES OF BANK CUSTOMERS
(account closures per six months)

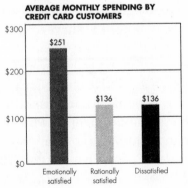

AVERAGE MONTHLY SPENDING BY CREDIT CARD CUSTOMERS

brains of customers who had the strongest levels of emotional attachment to the retailer were significantly more active while the subjects were thinking about the company. The increased activity was concentrated in parts of the brain related to emotion, emotional-cognitive processing, and memory. Moreover, the enhanced brain activity was company specific; customers who were passionate about the retailer but not the bank did not show the same enhanced levels of neural activity when thinking about the bank. (The attitude survey that had been used to separate the subjects into three groups proved to be a good proxy for the fMRI study, in that it reliably predicted which individuals would show the enhanced activity levels). Even more striking was the relationship between emotional attachment and self-reported share of spending, which were strongly correlated at 0.6 on a scale of -1 to +1. This suggests to us that there is an underlying neurological mechanism that links emotional attachment to subsequent behavior.

Clearly, a Six Sigma approach to measuring and managing the quality of the employee-customer interaction needs to take customers' emotions into account. Building on the work of psychologist Ben Schneider and management professor David Bowen, we have developed just such a measure of customer engagement. It combines traditional metrics of customer loyalty (overall satisfaction, likelihood to repurchase, and likelihood to recommend) with a short battery of items that assesses the emotional nature of customers' commitment. The first dimension it looks at is *confidence.* Does this company always deliver on its promises? Are its people competent? The second is *integrity.* Does this company treat me the way I deserve to be treated? If something goes awry, can I count on the company to fix it fast? The next element is *pride,* a sense of positive identification with the company. The fourth dimension is *passion.* Is the company irreplaceable in my life and a perfect fit for me? Truly passionate customers, by the way, are relatively rare. They are customers for life, and they are worth their weight in gold.

Our research suggests that for all kinds of companies, fully engaged customers—those who score in roughly the upper 15 percent to 20 percent on our measure—deliver a 23 percent premium over the average customer in terms of share of wallet, profitability, revenue, and relationship growth. Actively disengaged customers—those who score in the bottom 20 percent to 30 percent—represent a 13 percent discount on the same measures. And within a given company, business units whose levels of customer engagement are in the top 25 percent tend to outperform all other units on measures of profit contribution, sales, and growth by a factor of 2:1.

EMPLOYEE ENGAGEMENT

Every interaction an employee has with a customer represents an opportunity to build that customer's emotional connection—or to diminish it. Obviously, these interactions are not the only way to the customer's heart, but they are a large and largely untapped resource. In the United States, just 29 percent of employees are energized and committed at work, according to Gallup Poll data. Perhaps more distressing is that 54 percent are effectively neutral—they show up and do what is expected, but little more. The remaining employees, almost two out of ten, are disengaged.

Work groups whose members are positively engaged have higher levels of productivity and profitability, better safety and attendance records, and higher levels of retention. Not surprisingly, they're also more effective at engaging the customers they serve. Disengaged employees have a profound impact, too. We estimate that they cost companies $300 billion per year in lost productivity in the United States alone. They also destroy customer relationships with remarkable facility, day in and day out.

Performance metrics that acknowledge the importance of emotional engagement—on the part of both customers and employees—provide much stronger links to desired financial and operational outcomes. But deciding which metrics to use is just the first step toward effective management of the employee-customer encounter. Deciding *how* to deploy them is equally important. Unfortunately, in many companies, metrics designed with the right intentions are often deployed in the wrong ways.

The Encounter Must Be Measured Locally

We have all seen the claims: A major airline touts itself as an industry leader in on-time performance and has the flight departure and arrival data to prove it. A cellular provider claims to be a leader in customer satisfaction, citing an independent study of customers. A retailer announces that it has won an award for being one of the country's best places to work for the fifth year in a row. Each of these summary claims—based on the results of surveys—may be legitimate, but quick reviews of the on-time performance of specific flights, or candid conversations with cellular customers, or visits to several stores in the retail chain, inevitably reveal a considerable range of performance hidden behind the averages. Some flights are never on time; some always are. Some customers experience nothing but problems; others are routinely delighted. And some stores are exceptional places to work, while others are awful. High-level averages of company performance may provide good marketing copy, and they may make executives feel better about their position in the marketplace. But because they obscure the considerable variation from location to location within a company, they don't give managers and executives the information they need to improve performance.

Local variability shows up on virtually every performance metric we have examined. And it tends to be vast. In fact, the variations within a company easily dwarf the differences between competitors. Also, performance roughly follows a normal distribution, suggesting that local variability is largely unmanaged. (See the exhibit "It All Depends on Which Store You're In.") For sales and service organizations, unmanaged variability in the quality of the customer experience represents a significant threat to the enterprise's sustainability, because customers experience variation, not averages. Exactly the same pattern of performance variability emerges on employee measures, as well, with similar implications.

The only way to improve local performance is to provide feedback at the level where the variability originates. Suppose that instead of assessing your own heart rate, your physician based treatment on a measurement of the average heart rate for your entire town. It sounds absurd, but in many companies, something akin to this happens every day. The employee-customer encounter is assessed at the wrong level of specificity for the measurement to be useful. What does a cellular provider's description of itself as "an industry leader in customer satisfaction" mean to a customer who is routinely confronted with subpar service at a local level? And what does a company's label as "one of the country's best places to work" mean to an employee whose local workplace is miserable and depressing?

When the employee-customer encounter is assessed at the level of the local work group, executives can learn a lot about organizational performance. Let's say you manage one of several customer service call centers operated by a large telecommunications provider that we'll call Telecom A. Like its sibling centers, yours is a state-of-the-art facility, with an integrated CRM system that allows your CSRs to access each customer's relationship with the company—including account activity, rev-

---

It All Depends on Which Store You're In

Levels of customer engagement vary widely across the 1,100 stores of a retail chain we studied. Each bar represents the number of stores that fall into one of 28 customer-engagement performance bands, with poorly performing stores on the left and exceptional performers on the right. The top stores' performance is 3.5 times as strong as the poorest stores'. The shape of the curve (a normal distribution) suggests that the variability is unmanaged.

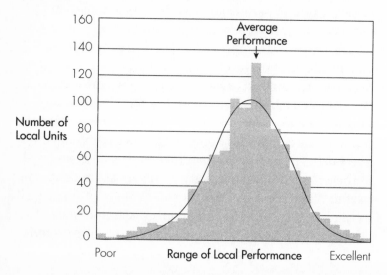

enue, and profitability—in real time. Calls are routed automatically to make the most efficient use of capacity. Every CSR is comprehensively trained, monitored, and coached, and there's little variation in the reps' pay from center to center.

To assess how well it is meeting its customers' requirements, Telecom A measures satisfaction at the company level by regularly surveying, and providing feedback from, a random sample of people who have recently called. Telecom A also conducts an annual employee survey. When you receive your copy of the quarterly customer satisfaction scorecard, you find that 88 percent of callers were satisfied with the service they received. The employee survey, meanwhile, reveals that just 40 percent of workers companywide feel they are adequately compensated. What exactly does this information tell you? Not very much. To truly understand the totality of the employee-customer encounter, you need metrics that go deeper into the organization. Fortunately, Telecom A has deployed just such metrics, and they have produced some startling insights.

One insight—and this is borne out by one of the largest CSR-level studies ever conducted (including some 5,000 reps)—is that the customer's experience still depends almost entirely on the particular rep who takes the call. The best 10 percent of CSRs produce six positive interactions for every negative one, based on postcontact interviews with customers. The worst 10 percent yield only three positive for every four negative encounters. Critical information of this type was hidden behind the overall summary score of 88 percent customer satisfaction. Without the deeper metrics, you as a call center manager would have been unable to identify or manage the sources of both poor and exceptional performance.

Or consider Bank B. Some time ago, its top executives recognized that employees affect profitability through two separate paths. The first might be described as *direct cost efficiencies.* Committed employees generate greater output at a higher quality level than uncommitted workers. They also stay longer with the firm, reducing training and replacement expenses. These efficiencies translate directly into enhanced profitability. The second path could be called *indirect customer outcomes.* Productive and committed employees generate stronger customer connections, which lead to higher levels of customer retention, profitability, and growth.

Early in their efforts to understand how to boost employee productivity and commitment, Bank B executives routinely assessed workers' opinions by surveying a random sample. They hoped to identify a key set of issues that, if improved, would make employees happier and more productive. The results were disappointing. It was not until they assessed worker attitudes at the branch level that they started to make progress. At the branches, employee attitudes ran the gamut from delight to disgust. Because Bank B measured at the correct level of specificity, it discovered that some local work groups epitomized the highest standards of excellence, while others were totally demoralized.

Local performance variation is the scourge of organizations that aspire to high performance. While it is in the nature of performance distributions to show variation (after all, "average" is simply a summary that represents almost no one's actual experience), the magnitude of the variability is a critical measure of organizational health. More than two decades ago, W. Edwards Deming and Joseph Juran noted that variability on critical performance metrics is a threat to the vitality of an enterprise because it is evidence that the business is not being managed effectively. And intuitively, it makes sense that the greater the range of performance on critical performance measures, the more costly the business is to operate.

Unfortunately, in most organizations, variability in the effectiveness of the employee-customer encounter goes largely undiagnosed. As a result, revenues and profits are bled off, and growth is anemic. The extensive range of local performance variation that exists in every company we've studied means that there is really no such thing as a single corporate culture or unified brand. There are as many cultures and "brands" as there are local work groups and customer touch points.

Local managers sometimes blame variability from location to location on factors such as store size, age, or locale that are beyond their control. Our research doesn't back them up. For example, within a chain of retail stores, controlling for those and other "immutable" variables—including local demographics and the presence or absence of competitors—eliminates only a portion of the performance variation among stores.

What explains this local variability? We've controlled for the factors that can't be changed. And the factors that are common across the enterprise—product, price, processes, policies, and so forth—can't, by definition, explain local variability (they often play a critical role in driving customer engagement, of course). If these factors don't differ from place to place, the only remaining culprit is the way those processes and policies are implemented locally. But that brings us to a consideration of exactly who is doing the implementing and how the implementation is being managed. To reduce variability in the customer experience, businesses must focus on reducing variability in local "people" processes (the "who" and "how" of implementation). The power of a local focus on reducing variability lies in its simplicity and flexibility. Each unit can identify and correct its own problems.

The Link to Financial Vitality

Conventional analyses of employee attitudes, customer requirements, and financial performance have emphasized the linearity of the relationships among them: Employee attitudes affect customer attitudes, and customer attitudes affect financial performance. We believe that the three factors also interact in complicated ways. Our Human Sigma metric combines employee and customer engagement into a single measurement that, we believe, provides a more comprehensive way of capturing and understanding this dynamic system.

The Human Sigma model grew out of a partially failed experiment. Several years ago, we were working with a large, multisite retailer on two separate initiatives to measure and improve its relationships with its employees and its customers. By surveying all workers as well as a sample of customers at each store, we were able to provide metrics for both relationships at the local level. We also found, not too surprisingly, that scores on both measures were strongly linked to the stores' financial performance.

As the project evolved, we wanted to understand what the top performers on each measure did differently from their less-stellar counterparts. We first identified the ten highest-performing stores on the basis of employee engagement, then did the same for customer engagement. Our working assumption was that at least a few of the top employee-engagement stores would also be top

customer-engagement stores. We were wrong. Just one
store appeared on both lists.

As we thought about that finding, we returned to the
data and noticed two things: As we expected, stores that
performed well (defined as simply being in the top half,
rather than the top ten) on both employee and customer
engagement produced considerably better financial
results than those that did poorly on both measures. But
stores that performed well on both metrics also outperformed stores that scored high on one but not the other.
This observation suggested that customer and employee
engagement interact to promote financial performance.

Our subsequent research has confirmed that customer and employee engagement augment each other at
the local level, creating an opportunity for accelerated
improvement and growth of overall financial performance. Our meta-analysis of the financial performance
of the 1,979 business units in the ten companies in our
present study reveals that local business units that score
above our database median on both employee and customer engagement metrics are, on average, 3.4 times
more effective financially (in terms of total sales and revenue, performance to target, and year-over-year gain in
sales and revenue) than units that rank in the bottom
half on both measures. The doubly stellar units are also
roughly twice as effective financially as units that are
high performers on one—but not both—of these critical
vital signs. In one luxury retail chain, for example, the
stores that scored high on both measures generated an
average of $21 more in earnings per square foot of retail
space than the remaining stores—a difference that translated into more than $32 million in additional annual
profits for the entire chain. The exhibit "The Interaction
of Employee and Customer Engagement" shows how the

average net gain per business unit is associated with low and high engagement of workers and customers.

As we have refined the Human Sigma concept, we have developed a method for combining employee and customer engagement scores at the local unit level to yield a single score that is reliably related to the unit's overall financial vitality. (See the sidebar "The Math Behind the Human Sigma Score.") This score allows us to classify units into six broad performance levels. Units in the lower two levels are in dire need of improvement:

The Interaction of Employee and Customer Engagement

Local business units with even moderately high levels of both worker and customer engagement are, on average, more effective financially than units with very high levels of only one form of engagement.

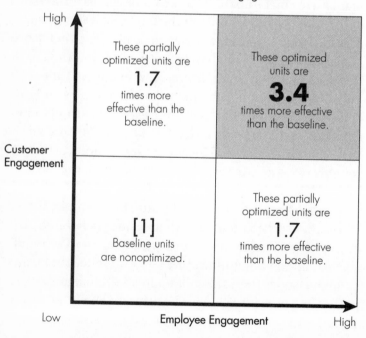

Those that engage employees without engaging customers have become too inwardly focused and have lost direction. Those that engage customers without engaging employees are living on borrowed time; over the long term, customer engagement will tend to erode. We consider units in the top three levels to be optimized. Obviously, we believe that sales and services companies

The Math Behind the Human Sigma Score

A business unit's Human Sigma score is computed by first converting its mean scores on employee and customer engagement into percentile equivalents (based on the observed distribution of scores for each metric). If a unit's converted scores on both metrics are above the median value for the distribution, the Human Sigma score is the square root of the product of the two percentile values, corrected for certain boundary conditions. (This correction value is equivalent to the ratio of the two percentiles—highest over lowest—raised to the 0.125 power.) If a unit's converted score on either metric is below the median value for the distribution, the Human Sigma score is the square root of the product of the two percentile values divided by 2. This produces a single bimodally distributed score that is then used to establish threshold values that define each of six Human Sigma levels, HS1 through HS6. The HS4 threshold is defined at 50. The HS3 threshold is defined as one standard deviation (SD) below that (using the standard deviation of the Human Sigma score distribution). The HS5 threshold is defined as one SD above the HS4 threshold. Successive thresholds are one SD away from the adjacent level. In algebraic terms: If employee engagement percentile and customer engagement percentile are both above 50, then:

$$HS = \sqrt{(EEpercentile \times CEpercentile)} \times \left(\frac{percentile\ Max}{percentile\ Min}\right)^{0.125}$$

If either employee engagement percentile or customer engagement percentile is less than or equal to 50, then:

$$HS = \sqrt{\frac{(EEpercentile \times CEpercentile)}{2}}$$

should strive to move all of their local units into the top performance level. This means that, over time, local performance variability must be reduced and overall performance increased. While difficult, such improvement is indeed possible. And the movement of units into successively higher Human Sigma levels brings with it enhanced financial performance.

How to Get There

A detailed look at how to manage and reduce variability at the local level would turn into a lengthy discussion, so we will make just three quick points.

Responsibility for Human Sigma must be centralized. Since employee and customer engagement are intimately connected—and since, taken together, they have an outsize effect on financial performance—they need to be managed holistically (at the same time that they're managed locally, which we'll get to in the next paragraph). That's easier said than done. In most companies, data about customers stay inside the marketing or quality department. Data about employee well-being reside, for the most part, in the HR department. And financial data, of course, live in finance. But only when these data are brought together on a single platform can a true picture of the health of the employee-customer encounter be drawn. It is simply not sufficient to provide managers with a "dashboard" of seemingly unrelated gauges and dials drawn from various and dispersed quarters of the organization. What this means in practice is that the responsibility for measuring and monitoring the health of the employee-customer relationship must reside within a single organizational structure, with an executive champion who has the authority to initiate and manage change.

The local manager is nonetheless the single most important factor in local group performance. Local-level managers have a huge role to play, for better or worse, in local performance. Earlier Gallup research suggested that employees join great companies but leave poor managers. That is, employees join a company for a variety of both high-minded and practical reasons. But, invariably, their working lives revolve around local environments that can either nourish them and foster their learning or starve them, causing them ultimately to leave the company—or to hang around, unproductively waiting for retirement. Local managers whose work groups show suboptimal performance should be encouraged to use the familiar tool kit of interventions: targeted training, performance reviews, action learning, and individual coaching. And managers themselves should be supported in similar ways. If none of these interventions leads to better performance, the local manager should be replaced.

Some companies will need to overhaul their HR practices. A set of longer-term, transformational interventions may be necessary in some instances. Executives or outside consultants may need to reexamine how local leaders do their jobs, how these managers are being developed, and how decisions are made and executed at the local level. If the Human Sigma numbers throughout the organization are lower than expected, or if parts of the organization sustain low numbers over time, then a broader intervention may be needed. The company may need to look at how it selects employees, promotes people into management, does performance appraisals, approaches succession planning, and recognizes performance.

Ask any chief executive to list his or her most pressing business challenges, and you will no doubt hear concerns about customer and employee retention, authentic and sustainable growth, eroding margins, and cost efficiencies. Clearly, there is no single solution to those challenges. But we are confident that measuring and managing two simple factors—employee and customer engagement—can lead to breakthrough improvements in all aspects of your business.

Originally published in July–August 2005
Reprint R0507J

Virtuoso Teams

BILL FISCHER AND ANDY BOYNTON

Executive Summary

MANAGING A TRADITIONAL TEAM seems pretty straightforward: Gather up whoever's available, give them time and space to do their jobs, and make sure they all play nicely together. But these teams produce results that are often as unremarkable as the teams themselves. When big change and high performance are required, a virtuoso team is far more likely to deliver outstanding and innovative results.

Virtuoso teams are fundamentally different from the garden-variety work groups that most organizations form to pursue more modest goals. They comprise the top experts in their particular fields, are specially convened for ambitious projects, work with frenetic rhythm, and emanate a discernible energy. Not surprisingly, however, the superstars who make up these teams are renowned for being elitist, temperamental, egocentric, and difficult to work with. As a result, many managers fear that if they force such people to interact on a high-stakes project, the group just might implode.

In this article, Bill Fischer and Andy Boynton put the inner workings of highly successful virtuoso teams on full display through three examples: the creative group behind *West Side Story,* the team of writers for Sid Caesar's 1950s-era television hit *Your Show of Shows,* and the high-powered technologists who averted an investor-relations crisis for Norsk Hydro, the Norwegian energy giant. Each of these teams accomplished enormous goals and changed their businesses, their customers, even their industries. And they did so by breaking all the conventional rules of collaboration—from the way they recruited the best members to the way they enforced their unusual processes, and from the high expectations they held to the exceptional results they produced.

BLOOD ON THE STAGE, racial tensions turned violent, dissonant music, and dancing hoodlums—*West Side Story* was anything but the treacly Broadway musical typical of the late 1950s. It was a high-stakes, radical innovation that fundamentally changed the face of American popular drama. The movie version earned ten Oscars. Not a bad achievement for the team of virtuosos—choreographer Jerome Robbins, writer Arthur Laurents, composer Leonard Bernstein, and lyricist Stephen Sondheim—who created it.

In nearly any area of human achievement—business, the arts, science, athletics, politics—you can find teams that produce outstanding and innovative results. The business world offers a few examples. Think of the Whiz Kids—the team of ten former U.S. Air Force officers recruited en masse in 1946—who brought Ford back from the doldrums. Recall Seymour Cray and his team of "supermen" who, in the early 1960s, developed the very first commercially available supercomputer, far outpacing IBM's most powerful processor. More recently, consider Microsoft's Xbox team, which pulled off the unthinkable by designing a gaming platform that put serious pressure on the top-selling Sony PlayStation 2 in its first few months on the market.

We call such work groups *virtuoso teams,* and they are fundamentally different from the garden-variety groups that most organizations form to pursue more modest goals. Virtuoso teams comprise the elite experts in their particular fields and are specially convened for ambitious projects. Their work style has a frenetic rhythm. They emanate a discernible energy. They are utterly unique in the ambitiousness of their goals, the intensity of their conversations, the degree of their esprit, and the extraordinary results they deliver.

Despite such potential, most companies deliberately avoid virtuoso teams, thinking that the risks are too high. For one thing, it's tough to keep virtuoso teams together once they achieve their goals—burnout and the lure of new challenges rapidly winnow the ranks. For another, most firms consider expert individuals to be too elitist, temperamental, egocentric, and difficult to work with. Force such people to collaborate on a high-stakes project and they just might come to fisticuffs. Even the very notion of managing such a group seems unimaginable. So most organizations fall into default mode, setting up project teams of people who get along nicely. The result is mediocrity. We've seen the pattern often.

For the past six years, we've studied the inner workings of teams charged with important projects in 20 of the world's best-known companies. We've found that some teams with big ambitions and considerable talent systematically fail, sometimes before our very eyes. In interviewing the managers involved, we discovered that virtuoso teams play by a different set of rules than other teams. The several dozen high-performance teams we studied, drawn from diverse fields, fit a few overarching criteria. Not only did they accomplish their enormous goals, but they also changed their businesses, their customers, even their industries.

Unlike traditional teams—which are typically made up of whoever's available, regardless of talent—virtuoso teams consist of star performers who are handpicked to play specific, key roles. These teams are intense and intimate, and they work best when members are forced together in cramped spaces under strict time constraints. They assume that their customers are every bit as smart and sophisticated as they are, so they don't cater to a stereotypical "average." Leaders of virtuoso teams put a premium on great collaboration—and they're not afraid to encourage creative confrontation to get it.

Among the work groups we studied were two from outside the mainstream business world—the creative teams behind *West Side Story* and the 1950s-era television hit *Your Show of Shows* and its successors. Both teams were vivid, unique, and, ultimately, managed to change their very competitive businesses. We also offer a more current business example from Norsk Hydro, the Norwegian energy giant. We intently studied a variety of sources, including diaries, interviews, video archive materials, and the impressions of many of the principals involved. In the following pages, we'll describe in more detail what constitutes a virtuoso team, how these teams work, and what they require in the way of leadership.

Assemble the Stars

Most traditional teams are more concerned with doing than with thinking. In other words, the working assumption is that execution is more important than generating breakthrough ideas. Team assignments, therefore, fall to people who seem to be able to get the work done. A less conventional approach, however, is more likely to produce exceptional results.

In virtuoso teams, thinking is more important than doing: Individual members are hired for their skills and their willingness to dive into big challenges. Instead of assembling a variety of individuals and averaging their talents down to a mean, virtuoso team leaders push each player hard to reach his or her potential within the overall context of the team objective. Virtuoso team members are not shy; they typically want to take on a risky venture that can pull them away from their well-trodden paths. They love daunting challenges, and they accept the risk of exposure and career damage if their projects fail. The risk increases pressure on the team to deliver; accordingly, the individual members give their utmost to assure that radical innovation happens.

If you want great performances of any type, you have to start with great people. In 1949, a young comic named Sid Caesar distanced himself from his competition by relying on a group of virtuoso writers including Neil Simon, Mel Brooks, Carl Reiner, and Woody Allen. *Your Show of Shows* and Caesar's other weekly productions were the biggest commercial successes on TV at the time. Week after week over a period of nine years, Caesar and his cadre of writers created live, consistently award-winning performances in a string of TV comedy hits. Mel Brooks famously likened the group to a World Series ball club, echoing the sentiments of many who acclaimed the team as the greatest writing staff in the history of television.

They may have been the best comedy writers in America—but they weren't the nicest. As is the case with all virtuoso teams, Caesar's staffers engaged daily in high-energy contests. It was as if each writer knew he or she was the best; every day, each tried to top the others for the "best of the best" title. The interpersonal conflict often intensified as the writers jostled aggressively to see whose ideas would be accepted. Mel Brooks frequently irritated Max Liebman, producer of the *Admiral Broadway Revue* and *Your Show of Shows,* and vice versa: Liebman found Brooks arrogant and obnoxious, while Brooks, for his part, declared that he owed no allegiance to Liebman. The tension among team members led Caesar to describe the competitive atmosphere as one filled with "electricity and hate"; two other virtuosos translated Caesar's description into terms of "competition" and "collaboration."

The *West Side Story* group was also famously discordant. To build the team, Jerome Robbins, a young classical ballet choreographer with an impressive résumé, sought out Leonard Bernstein, one of the moving forces in classical music composition and conducting; Arthur

Laurents, a highly regarded and successful screenwriter; and budding lyricist Stephen Sondheim. All of these talented players had enormous egos and greedy ambition. In their very first meeting, Laurents refused to play a subordinate role to the famously egotistical Bernstein, insisting vociferously that he was not about to write a libretto for any "goddamned Bernstein opera." All the team members engaged in similarly nasty tugs-of-war with one another. They needed each others' skills, not peace and quiet.

Build the Group Ego

Traditional teams typically operate under the tyranny of the "we"—that is, they put group consensus and constraint above individual freedom. Team harmony is important; conviviality compensates for missing talent. This produces teams with great attitudes and happy members, but, to paraphrase Liebman, "from a polite team comes a polite result."

When virtuoso teams begin their work, individuals are in and group consensus is out. As the project progresses, however, the individual stars harness themselves to the product of the group. Sooner or later, the members break through their own egocentrism and become a plurality with a single-minded focus on the goal. In short, they morph into a powerful team with a shared identity.

Consider how Norsk Hydro used a virtuoso team to handle a looming investor relations crisis. In 2002, Bloc 34, the potential site for a big oil find in Angola, turned out to be dry. Hydro had made a serious investment in the site. Somehow, senior management would have to convincingly explain the company's failure to the financial markets or Hydro's stock could plummet.

The senior managers understood that this problem was too critical to leave to conventional approaches, but Hydro was certainly not a natural environment for a virtuoso team. Rich in heritage, unwieldy, and traditional, with a strong engineering culture and a decidedly Nordic consensus-driven approach to decisions, the company never singled out or recognized individual performers. In fact, most of Hydro's business activities were specialized and separated. Teamwork was satisfactory but unexceptional, and tension among employees was firmly discouraged.

Defying precedent, team leader Kjell Sunde assembled a high-powered group comprising the very best technical people from across the company. Their task? To review a massive stream of data—one that had occupied the minds of some of the best professionals for more than four years. Their goal? To understand what had gone wrong in the original analysis of Bloc 34 and to assure key stakeholders that the company would prevent such an outcome from occurring again. Their deadline? A completely unreasonable six weeks.

Sunde's challenge was to strike a delicate balance between stroking the egos of the elites and focusing them on the task at hand. Each of the brilliant technologists was supremely confident in his abilities. Each had a reputation for being egocentric and difficult. Each had a tendency to dominate and aggressively seek the limelight. In a consensus-driven company like Hydro, the typical modus operandi would have been to exhort the individuals to surrender their egos and play nicely together.

But Sunde went in the opposite direction, completely breaking with corporate culture by publicly celebrating the selected members and putting them squarely in the spotlight. The Bloc 34 Task Force, nicknamed the "A-team," established a star mentality from its very inception. Selection for the project was clearly a sign of trust in each member's ability to perform outstanding work on a seemingly impossible task. For the most part, the members knew one another already, which eliminated the need for them to build polite relationships and helped them jump in right away.

Sunde then set about building the A-team's group ego. He guaranteed the members the respect they craved by assuring them that they would work autonomously— there would be no micromanagement or intrusive scrutiny from above. Team members would have absolute top priority and access to any resources they required, their conclusions would be definitive, and there would be no second-guessing. All this set a positive tone and bolstered group morale.

Still, there were plenty of early clashes. To control the friction, Sunde introduced an overall pattern to the teamwork. First, he paired off individual team members in accordance with their expertise and his sense of their psychological fit. Each half of the couple worked on a separate but related problem, and each pair's problem set fit together with the other sets to form the overall puzzle, which team members had to keep in mind as they worked.

Eventually, each team member understood that if the team failed, he would fail too. This kept any of the members from developing an entrenched sense of idea ownership. As it worked, the team transformed itself from a collection of egocentric individuals into one great totality. Had the group started out as a cohesive whole, individual talents might never have been realized and harnessed to the goal.

Make Work a Contact Sport

Typical teams are all too often spatially dispersed—they are managed remotely and get together only occasionally for debate and discussion. Most of the time, such a scenario works quite well. But when big change and high performance are required, these standard working conditions fall short of the mark. In virtuoso teams, individual players energize each other and stimulate ideas with frequent, intense, face-to-face conversations, often held in cramped spaces over long periods of time. The usual rounds of e-mails, phone calls, and occasional meetings just don't cut it.

When virtuoso teams are in action, impassioned dialogue becomes the critical driver of performance, not the work itself. The inescapable physical proximity of team members ensures that the right messages get to the right people—fast. As a result, virtuoso teams operate at a pace that is many times the speed of normal project teams.

Your Show of Shows and Caesar's other TV programs were developed each week in a small, chaotic suite of rooms on the sixth floor of 130 West 56th Street in Manhattan. Experimentation and rapid prototyping were the name of the game; only the best ideas survived. One team member compared the daily atmosphere to a Marx Brothers movie: People shouted at the top of their lungs; piles of food and cigarette butts lay everywhere. The pace was dizzying, yet everyone stayed focused. The pressure-cooker environment resulted in fierce interpersonal clashes, but there wasn't time to sulk or stay angry. The tight work space and relentless deadlines created a cauldron of energy and a frenzy of ideas.

Members of Norsk Hydro's A-team joked that they were not a task force; rather, they were "forced to task." Sunde established a dedicated room for the team and filled it with computer workstations and other necessary scientific and communications equipment. The space functioned both as a workroom and as a common meeting place (members of the team spent as much as 90 hours per week together). The atmosphere was relaxed and informal, and the discussions that took place there were open, honest, and passionate. Team members "would continually interact," Sunde said, "bouncing ideas off each other and to a degree competing, or at least keeping their eyes on each other."

The intense pressure on virtuoso teams affects project duration as well. These work groups usually break up for one of two reasons: Either the sheer physical, intellectual, and emotional demands take their toll (though *Your Show of Shows* and the team's other comedy hits lasted for nine years, there was high turnover within the writing group) or the stars, who are always in high demand, find themselves drawn to other new and challenging projects. Still, as long as the team members remain passionately interested and feel they have the opportunity to leave a significant mark on their company or their industry, they will work long and hard.

Challenge the Customer

Virtuoso teams believe that customers want more, not less, and that they can appreciate the richness of an aggrandized proposition. Virtuoso teams deliver solutions that are consistent with this higher perception. The vision of the demanding customer becomes a self-fulfilling prophecy, for while competitors create diminished offerings for their clients, virtuoso teams redefine taste and expectations and raise the level of market acceptability.

Before *West Side Story*, Broadway musicals were typically limited to a conventional formula of nostalgia, comedy, and feel-good endings. They were easily marketable entertainment. A typical hit of the day was *Damn Yankees*, a musical about a baseball fan who makes a pact with the devil. There was no room for tragedy, social critique, or even art on the Great White Way.

Robbins, Bernstein, Laurents, and Sondheim believed otherwise, but few agreed with them. Getting *West Side Story* to the stage was a huge challenge because most producers thought the project too risky, dealing as it did with themes of social consciousness and racial violence. How could it possibly make money? As venture capital dried up, Robbins and the others persisted, laying their careers on the line to bring audiences something totally new, daring, and different from anything they had experienced before. The enormous success of their project vindicated them.

Sid Caesar similarly believed that nothing was too much for his audience. At a time when American TV was beginning its long slide into programming mediocrity, Caesar wanted to get away from the crude, pie-in-the-face, seltzer-bottle slapstick that he found degrading. In a turnabout from convention, he and his team regularly presented audiences with challenging material. Liebman put it this way: "We take for granted . . . that the mass audience we're trying to reach isn't a dumb one. It has a high quota of intelligence, and there's no need to play down to it. . . . We strive for adult entertainment, without compromise, and believe that the audience will understand it."

For Norsk Hydro, the "customers" were the equity market analysts. The team members' job was to manage the market's reaction; if their explanation was slapdash or incomplete, the company's market value would nosedive. Faced with a similar situation, most businesses would have tried to downplay the fact that a gigantic project had failed, offering a pallid apology and then weathering the ensuing storm. Some companies, however, are able to turn these incidents to their advantage. (In 1988, for instance, an Ashland Oil storage tank ruptured while being filled. Diesel fuel damaged ecosystems and contaminated drinking water. The company's full disclosure and aggressive cleanup efforts restored its good name.) Likewise, Norsk Hydro turned the Bloc 34 incident to its advantage. The thoughtful explanations the virtuoso team provided left market analysts impressed with the firm's ability to respond convincingly and quickly to market concerns. The company received kudos in the press and was spared from any serious financial erosion.

Herd the Cats

Most leaders of traditional teams—even those working on big projects—emphasize consensus and compromise. Their goal is to keep stress levels low, meet deadlines, and produce acceptable results. By contrast, leaders of virtuoso teams must be far more deft and forceful. Their goal is to help individual performers, and the group as a whole, achieve their utmost potential.

The worst thing you can do to highly talented, independent people is to constrain their expressiveness; you have to trust and encourage their talents. At the same time, however, a team made up of these individuals must meet strict goals and deadlines. Balancing the virtuosos' needs for individual attention and intellectual freedom with the uncompromising demands and time lines of a high-stakes project requires unusual skill. For this reason, leaders of virtuoso teams assume different kinds of roles, and use different management tools, than do leaders of traditional teams.

One way to manage a virtuoso team is to be a rigid—even villainous—perfectionist. Jerome Robbins was a perfect example of this. He combined the unforgiving discipline of a boot camp sergeant with an artist's attention to detail. He pushed, prodded, embarrassed, and demanded excellence from his people; he overlooked no detail in an effort to capture the cast's total attention. For example, he posted articles about interracial gang warfare on the theater walls and encouraged others to find and share similar reports. Each gang-member character had a biography—for the first time on Broadway, there was to be no anonymous chorus—and actors were forbidden to use any other names in the theater. Robbins segregated the cast into their respective gangs. "This stage is the only piece of territory you really own in this theater," he barked. "Nothing else belongs to you. You've got to fight for it." This sparked genuine antagonism between the groups, which imbued the final production with verisimilitude.

Needless to say, tensions ran high, and the stress on individual players was enormous. In the end, many cast members hated Robbins (one thespian observed, "If I go to Hell, I will not be afraid of the devil. Because I have worked with Jerome Robbins."). Still, his hard-nosed leadership won him great respect. Chita Rivera, who starred as Anita in the Broadway version of *West Side Story*, noted that ". . . if [Robbins] hadn't been the way he was, none of those people would have danced the way they did. None of them would have had the careers that they had . . . because people give up, we all give up, and we give up a lot of times too soon. He made you do what you were really capable of doing, something you never even dreamed you could possibly do."

Other leaders of virtuoso teams take the opposite tack: They strive for excellence by fostering a galloping sense of intellectual and creative freedom in individuals and in the group as a whole. Sid Caesar let his team members express themselves as freely as possible and encouraged creative pandemonium. Though the process might have looked chaotic to an outside observer—and to NBC's management—Caesar kept the group focused on the goal: to produce the very best comedy possible for each show. His team members would work shoulder to shoulder to write and rewrite the same scene many times in the same week—sometimes in the same day— in a frantic effort to perfect it through repeated testing. Ideas, situations, and lines would be tossed back and forth, and, though most would be rejected, a choice few would be accepted and pursued. In the brainstorming maelstrom, ownership of the ideas was difficult to pinpoint. This created a sense of mutual respect and unity in the group; the writers felt they belonged to something bigger than themselves. "He had total control, but we had total freedom," writer Larry Gelbart, a contributor to *Your Show of Shows*, said of Caesar's

Traditional Teams vs. Virtuoso Teams

Virtuoso teams differ from traditional teams along every dimension, from the way they recruit members to the way they enforce their processes and from the expectations they hold to the results they produce.

Traditional Teams	Virtuoso Teams
Choose Members for Availability	**Choose Members for Skills**
• Assign members according to the individuals' availability and past experience with the problem.	• Insist on hiring only those with the best skills, regardless of the individuals' familiarity with the problem.
• Fill in the team as needed.	• Recruit specialists for each position on the team.
Emphasize the Collective	**Emphasize the Individual**
• Repress individual egos.	• Celebrate individual egos and elicit the best from each team member.
• Encourage members to get along.	• Encourage members to compete, and create opportunities for solo performances.
• Choose a solution based on consensus.	• Choose a solution based on merit.
• Assure that efficiency trumps creativity.	• Assure that creativity trumps efficiency.
Focus on Tasks	**Focus on Ideas**
• Complete critical tasks on time.	• Generate a frequent and rich flow of ideas among team members.
• Get the project done on time.	• Find and express the breakthrough idea on time.
Work Individually and Remotely	**Work Together and Intensively**
• Require individual members to complete tasks on their own.	• Force members into close physical proximity.
• Allow communication via e-mail, phone, and weekly meetings.	• Force members to work together at a fast pace.
• Encourage polite conversations.	• Force direct dialogue without sparing feelings.
Address the Average Customer	**Address the Sophisticated Customer**
• Attempt to reach the broadest possible customer base; appeal to the average.	• Attempt to surprise customers by stretching their expectations; appeal to the sophisticate.
• Base decisions on established market knowledge.	• Defy established market knowledge.
• Affirm common stereotypes.	• Reject common stereotypes.

management style. This statement goes to the very heart of what it means to lead a virtuoso team.

Regardless of their personal approaches, all leaders of virtuoso teams exploit time as a management tool. At Norsk Hydro, Sunde used time in a very specific way. Because presentations were kept to a strict limit of 15 minutes, members used their allotment to maximum effect. And the time limit prevented the more aggressive members from imposing their points of view on others. The deadline pressure was so great that the team had no choice but to maintain its focus on the task at hand. As one technologist put it, the strong adherence to time "made everyone aware that they had to dance to the same rhythm."

COMPANIES IN EVERY INDUSTRY pursue ambitious projects all the time, tackling big product changes, new market entries, and large reorganizations. But when breakthrough performance is called for, it's clear that business as usual won't suffice.

If you want to stamp out mediocrity, remember the instructive lessons from Sid Caesar's writers' group, the *West Side Story* team, and Norsk Hydro's A-team: Don't hesitate to assemble the very best and let their egos soar. Encourage intense dialogue—and then watch as the sparks fly. If you allow the most brilliant minds in your organization to collide and create, the result will be true excellence.

Originally published in July–August 2005
Reprint R0507K

Managing for Creativity

RICHARD FLORIDA AND JIM GOODNIGHT

Executive Summary

A COMPANY'S MOST IMPORTANT ASSET isn't raw
materials, transportation systems, or political influence.
It's *creative capital*—simply put, an arsenal of creative
thinkers whose ideas can be turned into valuable products and services. Creative employees pioneer new technologies, birth new industries, and power economic
growth. If you want your company to succeed, these are
the people you entrust it to.

But how do you accommodate the complex and
chaotic nature of the creative process while increasing
efficiency, improving quality, and raising productivity?
Most businesses haven't figured this out. A notable
exception is SAS Institute, the world's largest privately
held software company.

SAS makes *Fortune's* 100 Best Companies to Work
For list every year. The company has enjoyed low

employee turnover, high customer satisfaction, and 28 straight years of revenue growth. What's the secret to all this success? The authors, an academic and a CEO, approach this question differently, but they've come to the same conclusion: SAS has learned how to harness the creative energies of *all* its stakeholders, including its customers, software developers, managers, and support staff. Its framework for managing creativity rests on three guiding principles. First, help employees do their best work by keeping them intellectually engaged and by removing distractions. Second, make managers responsible for sparking creativity and eliminate arbitrary distinctions between "suits" and "creatives." And third, engage customers as creative partners so you can deliver superior products. Underlying all three principles is a mandate to foster interaction—not just to collect individuals' ideas. By nurturing relationships among developers, salespeople, and customers, SAS is investing in its future creative capital.

Within a management framework like SAS's, creativity and productivity flourish, flexibility and profitability go hand in hand, and work/life balance and hard work aren't mutually exclusive.

A COMPANY'S MOST IMPORTANT ASSET isn't raw materials, transportation systems, or political influence. It's *creative capital*—simply put, an arsenal of creative thinkers whose ideas can be turned into valuable products and services. Creative employees pioneer new technologies, birth new industries, and power economic growth. Professionals whose primary responsibilities include innovating, designing, and problem solving—the creative class—make up a third of the U.S. workforce and take home nearly half of all wages and salaries. If you want your company to succeed, these are the people you entrust it to. That much is certain. What's less certain is how to manage for maximum creativity. How do you increase efficiency, improve quality, and raise productivity, all while accommodating for the complex and chaotic nature of the creative process?

Many academics and businesses have made inroads into this field. Management guru Peter Drucker identified the role of knowledge workers and, long before the dot-com era, warned of the perils of trying to "bribe" them with stock options and other crude financial incentives. This view is supported by the research of Harvard Business School's Teresa Amabile and Yale University's Robert Sternberg, which shows that creative people are motivated from within and respond much better to intrinsic rewards than to extrinsic ones. Mihaly Csikszentmihalyi at Claremont Graduate University in California has documented the factors that generate creativity and its positive effects on organizations, advancing the concept of "flow"—the feeling people get when their activities require focus and concentration but are also incredibly enjoyable and rewarding.

While most students of the creative process have focused on what makes *individuals* creative, a growing number of thinkers such as Andrew Hargadon at the University of California, Davis, and John Seely Brown, former chief scientist of Xerox, are unlocking the social and management contexts in which creativity is most effectively nurtured, harnessed, and mobilized. Eric von Hippel of MIT and Henry Chesbrough of the University of California, Berkeley, have called attention to the critical role played by users and customers in the creative process and to a new model of "open innovation." Duke University's Wesley Cohen has shown that corporate creativity depends upon a firm's "absorptive capacity"— the ability of its research and development units not just to create innovations but to absorb them from outside sources. Business history is replete with examples of companies—from General Electric and Toyota to the design-intensive Electronic Arts, Pixar, and IDEO—that have tapped into the creativity of workers from a wide range of disciplines, as well as the creativity of users and customers, to become more innovative, more efficient, or both.

Despite such insights and advances, most businesses have been unable to pull these notions of creativity together into a coherent management framework. SAS Institute, the largest privately held software company in the world, is a notable exception. Based in Cary, North Carolina, SAS has been in the top 20 of *Fortune*'s 100 Best Companies to Work For list every year it's been published. The employee turnover rate hovers between 3 percent and 5 percent, compared with the industry average of nearly 20 percent. The governments and global corporations that rely on SAS's sophisticated business-intelligence software are overwhelmingly satisfied: The subscription renewal rate is an astounding 98 percent. And in 2004, the company enjoyed its 28th straight year of revenue growth, with revenues topping $1.5 billion.

What's the secret to all this success? As an academic and a CEO, the two of us approach this question differently, but we've come to the same conclusion. SAS has learned how to harness the creative energies of *all* its stakeholders, including its customers, software developers, managers, and support staff. Over the past three decades—through trial and error as well as organic evolution—SAS has developed a unique framework for managing creativity, one that rests on three guiding principles: Help employees do their best work by keeping them intellectually engaged and by removing distractions. Make managers responsible for sparking creativity and eliminate arbitrary distinctions between "suits" and "creatives." And engage customers as creative partners so you can deliver superior products.

These principles are driven by the premise that creative capital is not just a collection of individuals' ideas, but a product of interaction. As University of Chicago organization theorist Ronald Burt has shown, long-term relationships between employees and customers add to a company's bottom line by increasing the likelihood of "productive accidents." Thus, when SAS nurtures such relationships among developers, salespeople, and customers, it is investing in its future creative capital.

Managing with a framework like SAS's produces a corporate ecosystem where creativity and productivity flourish, where profitability and flexibility go hand in hand, and where hard work and work/life balance aren't mutually exclusive.

Help Workers Be Great

Creative people work for the love of a challenge. They crave the feeling of accomplishment that comes from cracking a riddle, be it technological, artistic, social, or logistical. They *want* to do good work. Though all people chafe under what they see as bureaucratic obstructionism, creative people actively hate it, viewing it not just as an impediment but as the enemy of good work. Do what you can to keep them intellectually engaged and clear petty obstacles out of their way, and they'll shine for you.

STIMULATE THEIR MINDS

SAS operates on the belief that invigorating mental work leads to superior performance and, ultimately, better products. It does not try to bribe workers with stock options; it has never offered them. At SAS, the most fitting thanks for a job well done is an even more challenging project.

An *InformationWeek* survey of tens of thousands of IT workers confirms that theory: On-the-job challenge ranks well above salary and other financial incentives as the key source of motivation. This is no surprise—since the pioneering work of Frederick Herzberg, managers have known that learning and being challenged motivate workers more than money or fear of disciplinarian bosses. What's different about SAS is that it goes to uncommon lengths to find the right intrinsic motivator for each group of employees.

Artists are inspired by the desire to create beauty. Salespeople respond to the thrill of the hunt and the challenge of making their quotas. Whatever the particular incentives, companies can take steps to help employees realize their goals. To ensure that its salespeople could make their quotas, for example, SAS developed a product-knowledge management system and created the position of sales engineer. That person's job is to answer staff questions and solve technical problems, so the sales reps can spend more time chasing down leads and less time digging up product specs.

Since developers thrive on intellectual stimulation, SAS sends them to industry- and technology-specific conferences, where they can hone their programming skills and build relationships within the larger software community. SAS stages its own R and D expos, where

SAS developers share their work with the nontechnical staff. The company also encourages employees to write white papers and collaborate on articles and books in order to showcase their knowledge. And SAS maintains a healthy training budget so individuals can keep up with cutting edge technologies. When employees return to the office, they are energized to apply what they've learned to their own projects.

Another way SAS keeps employees engaged is by frequently updating their tools. With the most advanced third-party productivity tools on the market, it's hard to get bored. Homegrown defect-tracking tools and source-control tools are continually refined, as well, and help workers do their jobs efficiently. In all cases, form follows function. As much as leaders at SAS value technology, they strongly believe that it's people who make technology useful, not the other way around. If a tool is constrictive or makes people change their preferred ways of working, then it gets scrapped. The goal is always the same—to help workers be great.

That holds true for all types of positions. Everyone working on the SAS campus is an employee; the company doesn't outsource any job functions. Whether you're a chef or a programmer, a groundskeeper or a director, you are a full member of the SAS community, and you receive the same benefits package. SAS recognizes that 95% of its assets drive out the front gate every evening. Leaders consider it their job to bring them back the next morning.

MINIMIZE HASSLES

In the creative economy, time is precious. And as much as creative people like to feel challenged, they don't want to have to surmount unnecessary obstacles. The former situation inspires greatness; the latter, migraines—hardly an ideal condition for creative thought. So SAS takes great pains to eliminate hassles for workers wherever and whenever it can, both off and on the job.

People who are preoccupied wondering "When can I fit in time at the gym?" or "Is that meeting going to waste my whole afternoon?" can't be entirely focused on the job at hand. The more distractions a company can remove, the more its employees can maximize their creative potential and, in turn, produce great work. *The Oprah Winfrey Show, 60 Minutes,* and lots of newspaper and magazine articles have publicized the perks SAS lavishes on its employees, but the company isn't just doling out treats willy-nilly. There's a deliberate process for choosing which benefits to offer (or, put another way, which distractions to eliminate). First, by conducting annual surveys and fielding employees' suggestions, HR finds out what people need. Next, it determines whether SAS can reasonably meet each need, asking, "Will we get enough of a return in terms of employee time saved to merit the investment?" If the answer is yes, SAS provides the benefit. If it's no, the company explains why. Even when SAS says no, it earns workers' trust and respect by engaging in a dialogue rather than issuing a seemingly arbitrary decision.

SAS has said yes to quite a lot. On campus, it has medical facilities for employees and dependents. Additionally, there's a Montessori day care center, and children are welcome in the company cafeteria, so families can eat lunch together. There are also basketball courts, a swimming pool, and an exercise room on-site, all of which make it easier for employees to fit a workout into their day. The company's Work-Life Department provides educational, networking, and referral services to help employees choose the right colleges for their teenagers, say, or find the best home health aides for their parents. Massages, dry cleaning, haircuts, and auto detailing are offered on-site and at reduced costs. (But SAS doesn't have, for instance, a doggie day care center because the numbers didn't add up.)

Obviously, the perks cost the company something, but think about the net gain. Not only do the benefits make workers more productive, but they also help retain those workers, reducing the company's expenses for recruitment and replacement. SAS saves about $85 million a year in such costs, according to Stanford University's Jeffrey Pfeffer, a leading scholar of talent-based organizations. It takes roughly six months to get a new worker up to speed in terms of technical knowledge, but it takes years for the employee to truly absorb a company's culture and forge solid relationships. By retaining workers, SAS protects and continues to enrich long-standing relationships among sales and support staff, developers, and customers—and it is in these relationships that creative capital resides.

Of course, there are other, less tangible advantages. Having health care on-site, for instance, reduces the amount of time employees are away from work for doctor visits. And medical conditions are generally caught earlier—because if it's not a hassle to set up an appointment and there's no need to travel across town, most people will see a doctor in the earlier stages of illness. As a result, employee productivity is bolstered, and less time is lost for medical reasons.

Likewise, subsidizing two-thirds of the cost of day care is an investment for SAS, not an unnecessary expense. It helps parents afford to come back to work, which means both the company and the employees win. SAS acknowledges and respects that employees have lives outside the office. The corporate philosophy is, if your fifth grader is in his first school play, you should be there to see it. SAS has earned a spot on *Working Mother*'s list of best companies so many times that professionals are lining up to apply.

SAS takes equal care to reduce administrative and other on-the-job hassles for its employees. At SAS, you won't find two-hour weekly staff meetings slotted into everyone's day planner. People meet when demands warrant it, not because "it's time." The CEO has been known to stand up and leave the room when a meeting becomes unproductive. The informal culture fosters impromptu discussions, and one of managers' responsibilities is to make sure the people who need to be sharing information are talking to one another.

It's not just useless meetings that SAS is out to eliminate—it's also outdated beliefs about proper ways of working. Take the standard workday. Creativity is a fickle thing. It often can't be shoehorned between the hours of nine and five; the Muses don't always show up on time for appointments. It's more important to capture the innovative insight—whenever it strikes—than to keep rigid work hours. To support the creative process and meet the demands of family life, flexible workday guidelines encourage people to start each day at whatever time is best for them. Some SAS jobs do require set schedules. Landscapers, for instance, arrive at 6 AM to get the bulk of their work done before the sun gets too hot. But in general, flexibility is appropriate, and it yields more output from workers, not less.

Although the press has played up the company's 35-hour workweek, the truth is, employees often put in extra time to complete a project or fulfill a responsibility. But make no mistake: This is a far cry from some Silicon Valley start-up. The company actively discourages people from working 70-hour weeks. "After eight hours, you're probably just adding bugs" is a company proverb, repeated often enough by the CEO and others that managers take it seriously. SAS encourages employees to disconnect from work for a time and then come back recharged. Creative people can be trusted to manage their own workloads; their inner drive to achieve, not to mention accountability among colleagues, compels a high level of productivity.

We're All Creatives

Few companies place as high a value on an egalitarian work culture as SAS does. There's no artificial dichotomy between suits and creatives because everyone there is a creative. The fact that the CEO still writes code is well known, but all of SAS's managers do hands-on work. Gale Adcock, the director of SAS's on-site health care center, for instance, is a nurse practitioner who sees her own patients one afternoon a week. The willingness—even eagerness—of managers to roll up their sleeves and delve into the "real" work of the organization sends an important message: We are all on the same team, striving toward the same goal of providing a superior product.

The importance of that point cannot be overstated. Knowing that your boss thoroughly understands and respects the work you do—because he or she has actually done it—has many positive outcomes. In addition to feeling that your contributions are appreciated, you'll probably be less hesitant to ask questions, because you know your manager "gets it," and you'll have more faith in your boss's decisions. Business life abounds with stories about managers who've failed to earn the respect of professional, technical, and other creative employees: the university president with no scholarly credentials, the law school administrator who's not a member of the bar, the movie studio executive who provokes a rebellion among directors, actors, and other talent.

Because colleagues at SAS earn one another's respect by producing excellent work, not by having a position near the top of the org chart, people aren't overly concerned with titles. Consequently, it's not in keeping with the corporate culture to withhold constructive criticism of higher-ups or hide problems from them; doing so would just result in an inferior product. In fact, most of SAS's leaders have an open-door policy. People are free to pop in to talk over an issue or pitch a new product idea. And the CEO might stop by your office to ask you questions about the project you're working on.

As egalitarian as they may be, creative companies must find the right role for their managers. At SAS, that role is to spark the creativity of the people around them. Managers do that, first, by asking lots of questions. As Carl LaChapelle, director of the Display Products Division, explains, "If you tell everyone, 'Here is how to do it,' then all you are really measuring is their typing skills."

The managers also bring groups of people together to facilitate the exchange of ideas and to spur innovation. For example, a number of years ago, the CEO believed so strongly in the importance of creating Enterprise Guide—a Windows-based forecasting application for business analysts—that he moved developers from various units down to the basement of one building so they could collaborate on the project full-time. To help shepherd it along, the CEO kept a satellite office in this Skunk Works area. Having him there not only motivated the team but also broadcast the company's commitment to the effort.

Finally, the managers clear away obstacles for employees by procuring whatever materials they need. Larnell Lennon, who leads the software-testing team, describes his job as "Go get it, go get it, go get it." When his people come to him asking for a software package or financial support, he doesn't pepper them with questions. If it's a reasonable request, he takes care of it. He knows he doesn't have time for anything less than complete trust in his employees, and vice versa. If the outcomes aren't up to snuff, that's a different matter. But in his seven years in the position, he says, he hasn't been given one reason to mistrust his people.

That's not to say that SAS never has difficulties with employees. With its enticing array of benefits, SAS is bound to attract a few people who would rather enjoy the perks than do the work. The company uses rigorous hiring practices to prevent such candidates from getting in the door; applicants may have to wait months for a decision while the company conducts a thorough vetting.

Once they make the cut, they enter a highly collaborative work culture. And since peers as well as managers are technically savvy, it becomes clear pretty quickly when someone isn't performing up to expectations. That person is given a corrective action plan and can either try to improve his or her behavior in the next three months or leave immediately with a parting compensation package. Either way, the process serves both the company and the employee well. Some have described SAS's philosophy as "Hire hard, manage soft." But "Hire hard, manage open, fire hard" is more apt. SAS, in other words, takes a relaxed approach toward controls; but the culture is allergic to couch potatoes.

There's absolutely no penalty for making honest mistakes in the pursuit of better products, though. Experimentation is crucial for breakthroughs, and some paths are bound to be dead ends. In fact, senior research and development director Deva Kumar gets upset only when people *don't* do something, because stasis can't lead to new insights. A few years back, SAS announced a new video game division, and managers let developers migrate there. When the department ended up failing, the developers were welcomed back where they came from. Even though the initiative didn't succeed, it taught management some valuable lessons and reminded employees that their company supported them, earning their loyalty.

Keep the Customer Satisfied

So far, we've shown how SAS keeps workers stimulated and provides perks that make employees at most other companies green with envy. We've described a management system that builds collegiality and trust. In the business world, though, it all boils down to deliverables. There are plenty of companies whose supposedly enlightened, "new age" management policies led them straight to financial ruin—and where new management came in and imposed neo-Taylorist controls in an attempt to undo the damage. Ultimately, if you don't build a product that people want (or, better yet, need), you won't be around for long. Engaging customers—the final piece of the management framework—is what keeps SAS from turning into a country club for talented techies.

Every company needs a constituency that holds its feet to the fire. For publicly held companies, it's Wall Street. Sure, they have customers, too, but Wall Street is so quick and ruthless that, in practice, it's hard to do the right thing by customers if the Street wants something else. SAS needs discipline as much as any company, but being private, it gets that from customers. That has big advantages, the greatest of which is this: While the stock price just tells you thumbs-up or thumbs-down, a customer tells you why, and how to get better, and will work with you to improve. But because the message from customers is more nuanced, it can also be more ambiguous. It's important, therefore, for management to make sure people throughout the organization hear customers' voices loud, clear, and unfiltered—so they're as unambiguous as a stock quote.

Day in and day out, SAS gathers—and acts on—customer complaints and suggestions through its Web site and over the phone. The company also solicits feedback once a year through its Web-based SASware Ballot, which asks users about additional features they would like. SAS prioritizes complaints and comments and routes them to the appropriate experts. Problems and suggestions are tracked in a database. When it's time to develop the next version of software, SAS resolves all recorded glitches and incorporates as many suggestions as feasible. For most of the company's 29 years, it has implemented the top ten customer requests. It has taken action on approximately 80 percent of all requests fielded.

Additionally, SAS collects feedback at an annual users' conference, which is quite unlike the usual sales-pitch-in-disguise event. Jeffrey Pfeffer described it as more like a Grateful Dead show than a standard software-industry hole-mending session. What it is, really, is a hotbed of creative energy. It's a forum for two groups of mutually respectful stakeholders to challenge each other to improve and innovate.

Imagine for a moment the vast creative potential of millions of users—highly intelligent professionals hailing from diverse disciplines and 110 countries. (SAS provides software to 96 of the top 100 companies on the *Fortune* Global 500, and to 90 percent of all 500.) This is the biggest and best focus group that loyalty can buy. Since these customers have access to all the latest software on the market, they're in a unique position to think comparatively about what the product they need should do, as well as what it shouldn't do. According to SAS's marketing creative director, Steve Benfield, it's difficult to develop software "when you don't have some external validation of one particular set of ideas over another. . . . But finding out what resonates with those beyond the office walls—that's gold!"

Creative capital is generated every time SAS's employees and customers interact. Consultants and technical support staff don't just troubleshoot; they collaborate with users to invent new solutions. Salespeople don't just sell software; they build long-term relationships and, in the process, learn surprising things about their clients' needs. SAS might be the only company that prints the names of its software developers in product manuals. Customers can—and do—call them up. And because employee loyalty is so high, the developers actually answer the phone: They haven't moved down the road to start-up number seven.

In large part, SAS can thank its subscription-plan business model for these regular interactions between employees and customers, and for its relatively stable revenue flows in a volatile industry. Customer loyalty is so high that the company saves money on advertising and other sales efforts. As a result, fully 26 percent of SAS's budget gets channeled directly into research and development. The average for high-tech companies is 10 percent. A well-funded R and D department leads to better products, which leads to happier customers, which leads to—you can see where this is going.

Another factor in customer allegiance is SAS's devotion to creating bug-free products. Users of most software products have been conditioned to accept glitches as inevitable in new releases; imagine their surprise (and gratitude) when that isn't the case. Twenty years ago, a particularly costly coding mistake was made at SAS. The product was sent to market, and fixing the error proved to be enormously expensive for customers and technical support staff alike. Lesson learned. These days, SAS performs some of the most robust premarket testing in the business. Testing teams run through a product from a developer's standpoint, a salesperson's standpoint, and a customer's standpoint. If the product isn't painless to evolve, sell, and use right away, SAS goes back to the drawing board.

SAS doesn't waste time and money patching up what it could have gotten right from the start. An ounce of prevention is worth a pound of, well, tech support. That doesn't mean support people aren't needed. But those creative professionals should be spending most of their time working with users to find ways to make the products and relationships better, not untangling messes that could have been avoided. By all accounts, that's exactly what happens. The average wait time on the tech support line is 34 seconds. And more than three-quarters of customer issues are solved within 24 hours. These are motivated employees providing first-rate solutions to very happy customers.

THE CREATIVE ECONOMY IS here to stay, and companies that figure out how to manage for creativity will have a crucial advantage in the ever-increasing competition for global talent. We believe that executives can look to SAS's management principles for guidance in boosting innovation, productivity, and business performance. If you leverage the intrinsic motivation of creative workers by stimulating their minds and minimizing hassles; if you raze barriers between managers and workers by ensuring that your managers are creatives, too; if you tap into the creative talents of your customers instead of looking just to your workers for new ideas; and if you nurture long-term relationships with users and employees alike, you will increase your creative capital manifold.

There's a virtuous cycle in play at SAS. How quickly other corporations can readjust the way they manage their own creative workers will determine how gracefully we are all able to transition into the creative age.

Originally published in July–August 2005
Reprint R0507L

About the Contributors

ANDY BOYNTON is the dean of Boston College's Carroll School of Management.

CURT COFFMAN is a global practice leader in the Denver office of the Gallup Organization.

MARILYN DARLING is a researcher and consultant with Boston-based Signet Consulting Group.

PHILIP EVANS is a senior vice president in the Boston office of the Boston Consulting Group. He is a coauthor of *Blown to Bits: How the New Economics of Information Transforms Strategy* (Harvard Business School Press, 1999).

BILL FISCHER is a professor of technology management at IMD in Lausanne, Switzerland.

JOHN H. FLEMING is the chief scientist for customer engagement in the Princeton, New Jersey, office of the Gallup Organization.

RICHARD FLORIDA is the Hirst Professor of Public Policy at George Mason University in Arlington, Virginia, and the author of *The Flight of the Creative Class* (HarperBusiness, 2005).

JIM GOODNIGHT is the CEO of SAS Institute in Cary, North Carolina.

JAMES K. HARTER is the chief scientist for employee engagement in the Omaha, Nebraska, office of the Gallup Organization.

MICHAEL C. MANKINS is a managing partner in the San Francisco office of Marakon Associates, an international strategy-consulting firm. He is also a coauthor of *The Value-Imperative: Managing for Superior Shareholder Returns* (Free Press, 1994).

JOSEPH MOORE is a retired Army Colonel, and former commander of the 11th Armored Cavalry Regiment, the Opposing Force at the U.S. Army's National Training Center in Fort Irwin, California. He is currently a researcher and consultant with Boston-based Signet Consulting Group.

CHARLES PARRY is a researcher and consultant with Boston-based Signet Consulting Group.

ROBERT E. QUINN is the Margaret Elliot Collegiate Professor of Business Administration in the organization and management group at the University of Michigan's Ross School of Business in Ann Arbor. His most recent book is *Building the Bridge as You Walk on It: A Guide for Leading Change* (Jossey-Bass, 2004).

ROBERT SIMONS is the Charles M. Williams Professor of Business Administration at Harvard Business School in Boston. He is the author of *Levers of Organization Design: How Managers Use Accountability Systems for Greater Performance and Commitment* (Harvard Business School Press, 2005).

RICHARD STEELE is a partner in the New York office of Marakon Associates, an international strategy-consulting firm.

BOB WOLF is a manager in the Boston office of the Boston Consulting Group.

Index